Christians and non-Christians alike are coming to terms with the uncertainty of this life. But as we balance ongoing uncertainty with our unwavering call as Christians, here comes Amy and Lynn, trusted friends, to help with a fresh look at the ancient text of Esther.

From the narrative of a girl who is often reviled, Amy and Lynn skillfully yet gracefully show how much like you and me she is.

With humor and transparent authenticity, Amy and Lynn share their pitfalls as well as biblical principles which helped them grow spiritually through trying seasons of life.

As you read the scripture and allow them to read you, like Amy, Lynn and Esther, God will encourage, convict, and empower you to stand firm, regardless of the outcome. Wherever you are in your life, this must-do bible study is for such a time as this.

Karen McNary, Bible Study Fellowship:
Director of Global Cultural Engagement

Have you had struggles where God felt invisible, uncaring, and uninvolved? Me, too. Amy and Lynn tenderly reveal how God is always in control and show us ourselves in Esther's story. This Bible study will guide you from Persia straight to the place you call home, and help you hope in God's unwavering hand when he leads you out of your comfort zone into your calling.

Amy Lively, author of *How to Love Your Neighbor Without Being Weird*

As a Bible teacher and lover of Esther's miraculous story, I thought that I knew everything about the book of the Esther. Wrong! Amy and Lynn's new study provides fresh spiritual insights as well as humbly and lovingly raising the bar on Spirit-led personal application and spiritual challenge. Personally, I loved experiencing fascinating new "a-ha" moments every day of this study!

Barb Roose, Speaker and author of *Surrendered: Letting Go and Living Like Jesus; Joshua: Winning the* [illegible] her studies

This study is a mix of fun, insight, and a deep dive into scripture. What I love most is that it has the power to teach me today how to live as a woman of faith right now, and to make a difference in a world that God loves like crazy.

Suzanne (Suzie) Eller, author, Bible teacher, co-host of *More Than Small Talk podcast*

Although the book of Esther doesn't directly mention God, Amy and Lynn help you see His guiding hand throughout this young queen's journey. You'll find helpful insights, engaging questions, and new perspectives realizing the Lord at work in your own story as you turn the pages of this excellent Bible study.

Melissa Spoelstra, speaker and author of *Isaiah: Striving Less and Trusting God More*

If you're looking for the standard "Here's how to get through hard times, just look to God" answers, you've come to the wrong Bible study. *Esther: Seeing Our Invisible God in an Uncertain World* goes beyond the platitudes and dives into the messy, deep end of the pool. If you've been swimming in the deep end for the past couple of years, asking the tough questions, this book is for you.

Kathi Lipp, Bestselling author and founder of Writing at the Red House

Seeing Our Invisible God in an Uncertain World

Study Guide | Six Lessons

LYNN COWELL & AMY CARROLL

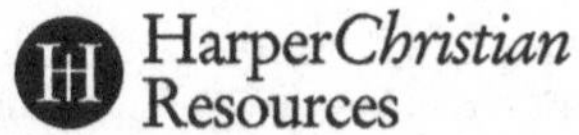

Esther

Requests for information should be addressed to:
HarperChristian Resources, 3900 Sparks Dr. SE, Grand Rapids, Michigan 49546

ISBN 978-0-310-14104-4 (softcover)
ISBN 978-0-310-14105-1 (ebook)

HarperChristian Resources titles may be purchased in bulk for church, business, fundraising, or ministry use. For information, please e-mail ResourceSpecialist@ChurchSource.com.

First Printing July 2022 / Printed in the United States of America

To our wise Umbrella friend, Suzie Eller.
Thank you for your continual love, support,
and cheerleading. You are the best!

Love, Amy & Lynn

Contents

Message from Amy and Lynn

DEAR NEW FRIEND (or maybe you're an old friend if we've studied together before!),

Thank you so much for your commitment to join Amy and me as together we go below the surface in the book of Esther.

Recently as my husband, Greg, and I watched another newscast of trouble in our world, overwhelm gripped me. *I have to do something! But what can I do? I'm just one person.*

I wrote that paragraph as if it was a one-time occurrence. It wasn't and it's not. That happened last night, but the reality is that this reaction to all of the uncertainty around us wells up in my heart often. One thing I am certain of, it will happen again.

So what do I do?

What do you do when the reality of the world's pain grips you? Shut off your heart? Move on? There is only so much heartache we can take.

One thing that helps me is a line I heard from Pastor Andy Stanley many years ago, "Do for one what you wish you could do for everyone."

This simple, but not easy, wisdom helps me, even today, as I ask the

Holy Spirit to direct me. I'll look for the way I can listen, feel, do, and speak and be an advocate for *one* today.

This pattern of listen, feel, do, and speak I've learned from Amy, and then even deeper from Esther as I began to study the book in the Bible with her name. It is a pattern that is serving me today and can guide me for a lifetime. I hope that as you study this book and the life of this woman, you'll find a way to move past *"But what can I do?"* to *"Let's do this, Lord"* with the encouragement you'll gain from Esther.

His,

Lynn

DEAR READER,

When Esther comes up in a group of women, inevitably I hear cries of, "Oh! Esther is my favorite book in the Bible."

I have to confess that I had never felt that way.

I mean, I never *hated* the book of Esther. I just didn't *love* it. Esther was never in my top ten favorite books of the Bible . . . or even top twenty.

While I adore all things feminine, I prefer a funky pair of sneakers over gowns and tiaras. Esther's story seemed too impossible to live up to. Too Disney princess to feel connected to. And conversely, the ending seemed too brutal to understand in my modern way of thinking.

But when an opportunity to write a study with Lynn Cowell, my dear friend and ministry teammate, on the book of Esther opened, I jumped at the chance! Between all my hesitancy about Esther and a finished manuscript, something amazing happened. I fell madly in love with both Esther and the book named after her.

The transformation started when Lynn saw that Esther walked through a process that God has been taking me through for several years. I've been going through these steps on repeat: Listen → Feel →

Do ⟶ Speak. When God opened my eyes to what Lynn saw (more about that in the study), suddenly I didn't see Esther as an unattainable model anymore. I saw her as a sister in the struggle to live as God's daughter in a really tough world. As a woman who cares about people and wants to do the right thing, the godly thing, as much as I do. As a woman who flounders a little in uncertainty but ultimately triumphs, bringing God great glory. I want that. Don't you?

Once I dove into studying Esther—a process that lasted for months—I found that I was converted. I now deeply love Esther and her true, gritty story. Whether this is your first time studying her story or it's always been one of your favorites, I hope you see Esther in the fresh light that God has shone on her for Lynn and me. And it's my deepest desire that God uses this study to ease your uncertainty and increase your confidence that you, too, have a significant place in His story.

In His Love,

Amy

Introduction

WHAT DO YOU DO when uncertainty strikes and God seems to have vanished? Our minds may tell us we serve an all-powerful God, yet our uncertain circumstances give rise to doubt when we can't *see* our invisible God.

Hi! My name is Lynn Cowell and more than once this has been the scenario in my life. My friend, Amy Carroll, has also experienced the same—times when our mind heads in a doubting direction:

Are You there, God?
Do You care about me and what I'm experiencing?
With all that seems out of control, are You really in control?

In uncertainty, wrestling with unbelief is a natural thing to do. As women who have spent years studying the word of God, Amy and I have come to the place where we now turn to God's Word when our minds wants to question what we cannot see.

This is why we've partnered together to write this Bible study. The book of Esther is perfect for us when we face uncertain times. Esther was a woman with little control of her own life, which feels very familiar to me. Esther carved a pathway for all women who find themselves walking through uncertainty. She shows us that we can do so, not only with faith but with influence.

As I read through the book of Esther, I saw a process emerging. A process Amy had shared with me months before in her own season of uncertainty:

Listen → Feel → Do → Speak

Within this time frame of Esther's story recorded here, God molded her into a woman who, though she may have been afraid of the uncertainty surrounding her, fulfilled God's assignment for her.

About the Study

As co-authors, Amy and I will both be contributing to the study content. As alternating authors, at the beginning of each week we'll share our names so you know who is teaching.

Each week includes five days of reading and reflection questions as we focus on this process of listen, feel, do, and speak. Before we dig into that process, we'll start week 1 with looking at our motives. We'll wrap up our time together in week 6, studying what our outcomes can look like when we follow through with the assignments God gives to each of us.

Each of the five days of study within the week will include portions of scripture from the book of Esther, supporting scriptures throughout the Bible, historical context gathered from study, plus reflection and application. We will study Esther's life and processes, while asking the Lord to take us on our own journeys through uncertainty so we can fulfill the assignments He gives to each of us.

We'll include a Pathway Principle at the end of each day to help you deepen and apply your study of Esther. At the end of the week, we'll give an overarching principle and a review of each day.

Memorizing God's Word

In addition to the Pathway Principles, there will be a memory verse that encapsulates the week's theme. Since many of us struggle with memorizing, Amy had the idea of giving unique and specific steps to help all types of learners to memorize. Give it a try! I did—and it works!

Options for Study

While we have designed this study to be used in your personal time with the Lord, we have also provided elements to make this study a resource for group study. At the end of each week, you will find group discussion questions providing a starting point for conversation and reflection. Some groups will find the setup of six weeks just right for the amount of time they have. Other groups may choose to divide the six weeks into twelve, providing more time for those who need it.

Additional Tools

In the back of this study, you will find an additional resource we have created to help you develop your own tool box for studying God's Word. I know you will find it helpful as you not only study Esther, but other books in God's Word as well.

Before We Begin

Studying God's Word is a very important practice for us as His daughters. It has the power to change the direction of each and every day of our lives. Before you begin, take some time to invite the Holy Spirit to be your teacher. In John 14:16, Jesus said He was sending the Holy Spirit to help us, and He has. If you have given your life to Christ, the Holy Spirit lives within you now. Ask Him to come and meet you each day, to teach you. Approach each day of study with a heart open to receive what He wants to show you and a willingness and intention to walk out His directives as well.

Lynn and Amy

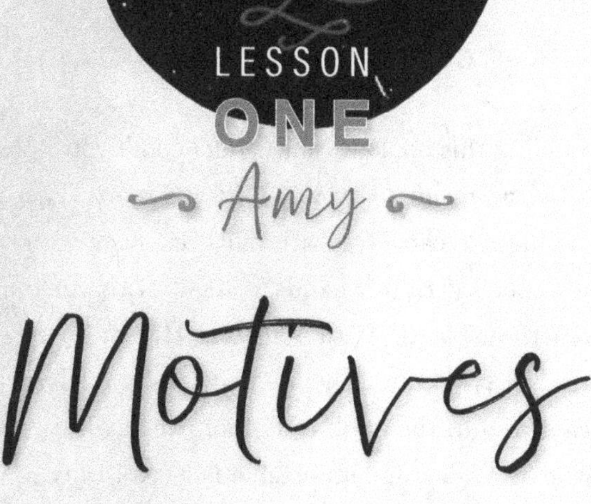

Day One: Tracing the Hand and Heart of the Invisible One

I stretched out on my single bed in my more-shabby-than-chic college apartment and stared up at the ceiling. Worry about final papers, end-of-semester exams, and where I'd head after graduation left me fuming and fussy. Finally, I exploded aloud, "I wish that God would just write me a note with all His directions, tie it to a rock, and then throw it through the window. I really want to know what *He* wants me to do!"

There was a pregnant silence across the room, and then my roommate, who had heard my rock-wish one too many times, answered with an eye-roll, "Oh, Amy . . . you know that if a rock came flying through the window with a note attached that you'd just run outside to see who threw it."

Sigh. She spoke the truth.

It's difficult to follow an invisible God in an uncertain life. We're just humans, surrounded by a physical world. The birds sing, and we hear their joy. The sun shines, so we see the glow and feel the warmth. The ice cream drips, and we take one long, delightful lick of strawberry. Our senses—seeing, hearing, smelling, touching, tasting—are the way we experience the world. Their input helps us to map out our next move, know whom to trust, stay out of harm's way, decide what to swallow or spit out, and discern when to run. Our senses are almost everything to us.

Almost.

If you're holding this book in your hand, I count you as a sister. There's a sacred place wired inside us to know there's more. There's something bigger than us that we can't see with our eyes, hear with our ears, sniff with our noses, touch with our hands, or taste with our tongues. It's not actually a "something" at all. It's a Someone. He's more magnificent than our senses—in fact He created them—and He's real. He's God.

Before we dive into the book of Esther, we have to wrap our hearts and minds around a very uncomfortable fact. Not only is God invisible in this book of Scripture, He's not even mentioned. Not named. Not once. Not. At. All. It's one of only two books in the Bible that never names God directly.

This gap has led to a lot of controversy swirling around the book of Esther. There are many interpretations of her story, but some thought it shouldn't be included in our Bibles at all. The absence of God's name was so disconcerting that many early Christian giants either ignored the book or spoke out against it. "For the first seven centuries of the Christian church, not one commentary was produced on this book. In fact, two of the biggest names in church history seemed to have major issues with Esther. As far as we know, John Calvin never preached from Esther. Martin Luther denounced this book together with the apocryphal 2 Maccabees, saying of them, 'I am so great an enemy to the second book of the Maccabees, and to Esther, that I wish they had not come to us at all, for they have too many heathen unnaturalities.'"[1]

That may be shocking to those of us who love Esther's story, but it's true. Luther wasn't wrong, was he?

1. No God-mentions
2. Lots of very flawed people
3. Set in a culture that didn't worship the one true God

The book with Esther's name on it doesn't sound like the ideal sermon series or a model of godliness for children. Even so, the book of

Esther is perfect for us today. As you'll soon see, she's a woman up to her neck in uncertain circumstances beyond her control and living in a culture that doesn't worship the way she does. Yet, she's part of a community who loves their invisible God. Feel familiar?

What do you find difficult in loving and following an invisible God?

____

____

____

____

____

____

____

____

This unique book is one of the rare books in the Bible without a known author. Most Bible scholars believe that the unknown author of Esther left God's name out on purpose as a literary device that forces us to search for God's hand. It's a genius move, but the writer wouldn't have expected us to see God in a vacuum with no context.

Throughout this study, Lynn and I will include tips that will equip you to dig deeper and understand Scripture more fully in your individualized study time. They are also compiled in an appendix at the back of the book.

I've given a name to one essential Bible study method that many scholars have used for centuries. I call it The Clarity Principle, and here's how it works. When we run across a difficult-to-understand passage of Scripture, we don't rush to interpret it through our human lens or build a wonky theology, a belief system about God, around it. Instead, we dig into the whole of Scripture, interpreting the unclear passages with the clear ones, thus The Clarity Principle. As we think about our invisible God, we know that He isn't *always* concealed as He is in the book of Esther. Let's use The Clarity Principle here for a moment.

Look up and read the following passages. Draw a line from the Scripture to the way that God has revealed Himself and/or His message to humans.

1 Kings 19:11–13	Fire
2 Chronicles 34:22–24	A prophet
Genesis 16:6–8	A donkey
Exodus 3:1–2	A whisper
Numbers 22:27–31	Angels of the Lord

God has made Himself seen and heard in varied ways, some quite surprising. These are only a handful of examples from the Old Testament!

Can you think of some additional ways Scripture tells us God makes Himself known? If so, list them here.

____

____

____

____

____

____

You may have listed visions (Genesis 15:1), dreams (Genesis 37:5), a voice from heaven (Matthew 3:13–17), or tongues of fire (Acts 2:3). Our God is so creative that we could list all day. Because of His goodness, He reveals Himself to us in many ways so that we *will* see Him.

Although God seems to have vanished in the book of Esther, He has never played a game of hide-and-seek with us. Jesus Himself, fully God and fully man, came to reveal God in a way that all our senses could experience. Those who walked with Him on earth could absorb His reality with their whole beings. Jesus is the pinnacle of how God has revealed Himself to man. In fact, Colossians 1:15 says, "The Son is the image of the invisible God, the firstborn over all creation." God has made His message and His character visible through His Son, Jesus.

Read these passages and list what each tells you about the character of God.

Exodus 34:6–7

Psalm 25:6

Psalm 147:5

Malachi 3:6

Job 19:25 (Don't miss this one! It's central to the book of Esther.)

This is only a partial list of the innumerable attributes of God. If some others come to mind, list them here.

____

____

____

____

____

Lynn recently sent me a picture of a cute sign in a shop that she frequents. It says, "Let our work speak louder than our talking points." This is a fervent prayer for me as a wordy girl at heart. But God already functions this way: His work reveals His glory. This is what we have to look forward to in this study.

There may be a silence as it relates to God's name, but His Presence shouts all the way through the book of Esther. Just like in the Song of Solomon, the other book that doesn't mention God's name, God is made visible through His fingerprints of love. There is a string of "coincidences" we'll trace too significant to be anything but a display of God's Providence, His protective care.

In this first week, we're taking a magnifying glass to the motivations of all the characters in this fascinating story, so let's start with God.

What *could* His motivations be in this book? They're not spelled out for us, and we should never presume to know exactly what God is thinking unless Scripture explicitly says it. Yet, His core motivations become very clear as we consider this book as one puzzle piece with the other sixty-five. Let's use The Clarity Principle again. God's motivation since the fall of man in Genesis 3 is to redeem, to rescue, and to restore all that is broken between Himself and those He creates and loves. What is His name that reveals His motivation in each of these stories?

For Noah's family in the flood (Genesis 5–8) . . . Redeemer.
For the Israelites coming out of slavery in Egypt (Exodus 2–13) . . . Redeemer.
For the weary exiles returning to Jerusalem (Ezra) . . . Redeemer.
Through Jesus on the cross (John 19) . . . Redeemer.

Throughout all of Scripture, God is consistently rescuing and redeeming. Let's watch closely as His undercover work reveals His pursuit of redemption all through the story of Esther.

There are two seemingly conflicting truths that are equally accurate:

1. God sometimes seems to have vanished.
2. He's always present even when we feel like He's left us.

Our invisible God never leaves us. But sometimes He's standing in our blind spot, beckoning us to watch for the effects of His hand.

That's what I want you to take away from our first day together, because *(spoiler alert!)* the focus and superhero of this book isn't the one with her name at the top. As in the rest of Scripture, the primary hero was and always will be God. He may not be named, but watching His every move in this story will teach us more about Him and how He is always, *always* with us even when we can't see Him.

Knowing whom He is helps us to more accurately interpret the actions of His unseen hand in this story. God is good. He is loving and trustworthy. Then and now, He always keeps His promises. He is the Redeemer who rescues those He loves.

Pathway Principle

God is faithful and ever-present, even when it seems He's vanished.

Memorize

"For since the creation of the world God's invisible qualities—his eternal power and divine nature—have been clearly seen, being understood from what has been made, so that people are without excuse" (Romans 1:20).

Read the memory verse aloud four times. Read it very slowly the first time and faster each subsequent time.

Application

Your one application this week is to read or listen to the whole book of Esther in one sitting. Depending on the rate at which you read, it will take you around forty-five minutes. Lynn and I want you to have an overview of the whole story from the very beginning. If this is the first time you are reading Esther, you'll see what an exciting part of God's story it is. If you've read it before, I guarantee you'll be challenged and inspired anew!

Day Two: For the Love of a Story

In my home state of North Carolina, tucked into the southern, coastal region of the U.S., natives are known for a list of cultural delights. Our food is second-to-none (we think!) with barbeque and sweet tea topping the menu. Accents here are as slow and warm as a summer's day. Our turns-of-phrase sprinkle conversations with colorful word pictures. And when we're in a house overflowing with people, you can count on my husband to shake his head and say, "Too many fleas on one dog!"

There's one love that trumps all the others in the south, though. We're a people with a full-blown obsession with a well-told story. One of my favorite field trips as a third-grader was our class trip to the storytelling festival on the lawn of Raleigh's State Capitol. My brain has a storeroom filled with vivid memories of small groups of kids sitting on blankets, legs splayed in all directions, as professional storytellers spun their yarns. We were rapt in the rare silence of children. Our imaginations were racing while our bodies were still. I attended that festival over forty-five years ago, but the girl inside is still transfixed by a great story.

I don't think it's just southerners who love a story. Humans have handed down stories, both fictional and historical, since the beginning of time. There's something in our souls that responds to a story written in a book, told by a friend, or recounted on the flickering screen of a movie theater. We love to watch heroes triumph, villains be vanquished, and happy endings emerge.

Stories can be enjoyed just for pleasure, but they also inspire and teach.

Make a short list of two to three stories of any genre that have captured your heart and mind. Put one favorite lesson beside the name of each story you've listed.

The great news about our study is that Esther is not just a captivating story. It's epic. And better yet, it's true. To understand the story of Esther, we need to understand all the elements: genre, time, setting, and characters. Without knowledge of these pieces, we'll lose the richness and nuances of this book.

Just like a human writer puts together a story, God is the author of this story. He chose and developed the characters, human free will and all. He divinely picked the setting. God's hand scripted each scene, and He determined the timing of each move. Our Redeemer didn't just craft a story in a fictional world like a human author. He created the story in our real world and brought about His ultimate good. Let's take a look.

How does picturing God as the author of this true story help you see His part in it?

____

____

____

____

____

____

____

The Genre

The Bible itself contains multiple genres, or types, of writing. There are narratives/histories like Kings and Chronicles. Proverbs and Ecclesiastes are wisdom literature. There are books of poetry, including Psalms, and prophecy like Jeremiah and Isaiah. In the New Testament, there are Gospels that tell the life of Jesus and epistles, which are letters that teach. When you're studying, it's important to know the genre of each book and take it into consideration. Knowing the genre helps us to understand and interpret Scripture. For example, similes in poetry aren't interpreted literally, they're word pictures designed to illustrate a concept or principle.

There is a lot of debate about the genre of Esther, but since I'm not a Bible scholar, I'm not going to go deep into all the arguments here. If you're interested, please use that spark of curiosity to dig into some of the resources we list in the endnotes.

In a nutshell, Esther seems to be a blended genre. It is history but told with the "artistry of great literature."[2] That's a contrast to the kind of reporting we'd find in a newspaper article. Instead of containing "just the facts, ma'am," Esther includes elements and details that heighten the unfolding drama. This is consistent with Hebrew narrative and how historians at the time wrote. It also conforms to the way we tell a story across the table to a friend. The retelling is true even though some details are left out and others are emphasized.

Narrative, or storytelling, has always been a powerful genre that can both inform and teach. The emotions evoked in a story can reform the listener. In this story, God, the author, establishes His love for His chosen people, the Jews, and His providential care over them.

In addition to genre, here's another Scriptural distinction that's important to understand. There are two main types of Scripture: *descriptive* and *prescriptive.* It's important to know the difference, because prescriptive Scripture contains directives from God.

Prescriptive passages tell us what to do and how to please God. **Descriptive Scripture** simply relates a story without commentary on the morality of the actions.

If we confuse descriptive and prescriptive Scripture, it can lead to interpretive trouble. I found this great question to help us tell the difference between the two types. "Is the passage *describing* something (it happened) or is it *prescribing* something (it should happen)?"[3]

The narrative in Esther isn't prescriptive. Instead, it's descriptive. One of Esther's unique traits is that the narrative is completely devoid of any discussion of motives, thoughts, or how God judges human actions. Much is described with no commentary as to whether God sees it as right or wrong.

How can it aid in your individual Bible study to know the difference between prescriptive and descriptive Scripture?

Read 2 Timothy 3:16–17. List the source and functions of Scripture that are revealed in these verses.

Think about the possible goals of the unknown human author of Esther. Circle words from the list you made in the previous question that could have been the author's possible goals for writing the book of Esther.

The Time and Setting

Hang with me through a lot of details here. I promise that some fascinating connections are coming.

Although we can't nail down the exact dates, they vary slightly according to the source, Esther became queen around 478 BC in the Persian Empire. If you look at the timeline, you'll see where this book falls in God's big story.

722 BC: Samaria falls, and the Assyrian exile of Israel begins
586 BC: Jerusalem falls and the Babylonian exile of Judah begins
539 BC: Babylon falls to Cyrus, king of Persia
537 BC: Cyrus makes his first decree (Ezra 1:1) and the first group of Jews return to Israel and begin to rebuild, the Postexilic period begins
486–465 BC: Xerxes' reign
478 BC: Esther becomes queen

Here's a summary of Israel's history during this time from a ten-thousand-foot perspective. The book of Judges documents the continuing cycle of sin and idolatry, which is the worship of other gods. God punishes the kingdoms, both Israel and Judah, that were once united as Israel by removing them from the land He had given them. Just like a loving parent, God's discipline was designed to bring His people back to Himself and into chosen obedience. Israel goes into exile first, taken by Assyria. Then Judah is conquered by Babylon and taken into captivity, a painful exile away from their God-given land.

Around forty-seven years into the Jewish exile in Babylon, Babylon is conquered by another power, Persia. The king of Persia, King Cyrus, seizes control. The biblical books of Ezra and Nehemiah are records of the Jews, the people from Judah, who began to return to Israel after Cyrus released and equipped them to go. For all of you who are word nerds like me, this timeframe is called the **Postexilic period** because it was *after* the *exile* was officially over. (Yes, friends, I *have* been practicing how to say Postexilic. It doesn't exactly trip off the tongue, but I desperately want to use it in a sentence.)

I know that's a lot, and you might be wondering where the fascinating epic-ness of Esther starts. With all the details, it's hard to synthesize them, but let's put it all together. The book of Esther covers about ten years during the rule of Xerxes, a king who reigned about forty-five years after Cyrus.

Bible Nerd Box

It can be confusing that different translations use different names. Xerxes is his Greek name, while Ahasuerus is the Hebrew variant. They're different names for the same king, so don't be confused if you have a translation that uses Ahasuerus or if you see it when we quote from the English Standard Version. Lynn and I decided to use Xerxes in this study because it's the version that we can pronounce.

Esther and Mordecai, the main characters whom we're about to get to in a moment, were Jews residing in the Persian city of Susa during a time when they didn't technically have to be there. Instead of going back to the Jewish homeland of Israel, they stayed in a pagan land where they were foreigners. Why?

Just like the name of God, the book of Esther is silent about their motivations in staying, but we can make some educated guesses based on a little history and a big understanding of our own human nature. Jerusalem was a pile of rubble at this point in history, but Susa was the winter home and playground of the royal family. Cushy much? Esther would have been born in Persia, so all the strangers weren't strange to her. They were familiar, and humans are always drawn to familiarity. Persia wasn't their historical home, but it had become home in every other way. There were families, houses, and livelihoods. No matter the exact human reason, God, our divine Author, had placed Esther and Mordecai in this time and setting.

Describe the time you live in:

____

____

____

____

____

Describe your setting (country, town, neighborhood):

Acts 17:26 says, "From one man he made all the nations, that they should inhabit the whole earth; and he marked out their appointed times in history and the boundaries of their lands."

What thoughts come to mind knowing that God chose the time and place for Esther, and He's also chosen the time and place for you?

The Characters

There are five main characters in Esther, and we'll give each of them the space they deserve in upcoming days.

King Xerxes	Queen #2 Esther	Haman
Queen #1 Vashti	Mordecai	

Just like us, each one of them has many layers. They're all very human with a full range of emotions and the choice to follow God or reject Him.

It's interesting to note that there's a turning point, a place of decision, for each character. This beautiful book shows both the Sovereignty, or rule and reign, of God as well as human choice as elements in God's bigger story.

Below, fill in the blanks with names of real-life people in your real-life world.

__________, __________, __________, and __________ are some of the characters that God has put in my story.

Our Motives Revealed

The story of Esther has been reviled at times, but it's beloved, too. Her story has been told over, and over again. Fictionalized accounts have been written, movies like *One Night with the King* have been made, and there are even cartoon versions. As the book of Esther has been Hollywood-ized, it's also been sanitized. Just like our Christmas nativities don't portray an accurate, Scriptural view of Jesus' birth, these renditions start to smudge our view of the whole of Scripture. Cleaned-up versions end up leaving us *with* what we wish but *without* what we need. Why do we always want to clean up God's story?

I've come to the uncomfortable conclusion that the motive for dunking God's Word into spiritual Clorox is that we don't want to face our own flaws. We'd rather skew Scripture than look at ourselves in the mirror displaying the weaknesses of the people He uses. Let's make a pact. Right here. Right now. Let's commit to reading and studying Esther minus our rose-colored glasses. Without our spiritual Clorox. Let's look at the hard stuff so that we can truly celebrate the beautiful work of God in the lives of messy humanity.

List two or three reasons that you think make humans want to "clean up" God's story.

What are the dangers involved when we do so?

One of the many beautiful characteristics of Scripture is that it's God's big story, populated with sinful humanity, told honestly. When we recognize God as both author and hero of His story, we can also begin to see His authorship in our personal story. Despite our flaws and failures, we are a part of God's big story. We can trust that our faithful Author is writing us into His amazing tale!

Pathway Principle

God is the author of our story.

Memorize

Today, write out the memory verse four times and then read all four times aloud. Circle words that are meaningful to you.

"For since the creation of the world God's invisible qualities—his eternal power and divine nature—have been clearly seen, being understood from what has been made, so that people are without excuse" (Romans 1:20).

Application

Have you read the book of Esther from beginning to end yet? If not, it's okay! It's your only application this week. Your assignment today is to schedule a time on your calendar to do it before the end of the week. It will take about forty-five minutes.

Day Three: When My "Why" Is Me, Myself, and I

During a polarizing election cycle, I opened my email and found a copy-and-pasted message from an acquaintance containing her beliefs about the times in which we lived. The message was long, full of error, and punctuated with undertones of hate.

To say that I didn't appreciate this email would be a grave understatement. I was furious. How dare she send me such a thing! The words assaulted my values and were a gross misrepresentation of the faith we share. So . . . (insert sarcasm here) I did what any good Christian woman would do. I composed a scathing social media post in my head:

> If you're someone who sends unsolicited political emails expressing your "concerns" to people that you haven't spoken to in years, I have a little advice.
>
> Stop it. Now.
>
> You're not changing minds OR winning hearts.

I. Was. Hot.

Thankfully, I paused before I posted, and God intervened through Scripture. Esther 1 is where God directed me, and as I read, I remembered an application that shone a spotlight on my anger and challenged my motives.

Read chapter 1 of Esther and jot down here what jumped out at you. Often the Holy Spirit will make verses jump off the page, or "come alive," when we need to apply God's Word to our own lives.

When I was a little girl, there was nothing that I loved more than dressing up. My mother lovingly created a dress-up box for me filled with her old dresses, discarded shoes, outdated jewelry, and a few costumes. I'd clunk around our house in oversized shoes all day long, adorned in sparkling "jewels" and dragging the "train" of her too-big dresses behind me.

At some point in every childhood, there's a dream to be a princess or Wonder Woman. We want to be part of a story in which the good guys win every time. There's a longing in the human heart to be a hero.

Just like you, I'd choose to twin with Esther in this story, but the day I received the email and read chapter 1, God used the opportunity to show me my likeness to King Xerxes instead. He used the Scripture to shine a light on my motives, and I didn't like what I saw.

The Root of Rotten Motives

In chapter 1, verses 1–8, the author describes the first character that we meet in the book of Esther, King Xerxes. A little of his personal history helps us make sense of this chapter. Xerxes was the son of Darius, a Persian king who perpetuated the ongoing conflict between Persia and Greece. Toward the end of Darius' life, he led a losing campaign against Athens, the capital of Greece, and died before he finished planning a second attack.

Herodotus, a pagan Greek author of the day who is often referred to as "The Father of History," recorded accounts of the Greco-Persian wars. In an account that verifies Scripture, he wrote that Xerxes held an enormous banquet to garner the favor and resources of his kingdom. The banquet was held to raise troops and funds for yet another war against the Greeks. Xerxes' aim was to avenge his father and restore glory to his present kingdom. This banquet Herodotus described is the same one detailed in the opening chapter of Esther.

The banquet included an extravagant timeline, lavish decorations, priceless table settings, sumptuous food, and an endless flow of booze. When we break down the king's motivation, digging deep into his "why," we can see two self-centered motivations.

King Xerxes had:

Something to prove—The king's banquet and the war he was planning were a show to prove that he was wealthy, strong, and worthy to anyone in doubt.

Something to earn—The banquet was also a means of earning support and finances from those attending or watching.

In both cases, Xerxes was not serving his people. All of Xerxes' actions were self-motivated.

When I thought about my root-motives for the social media post that I was considering, I realized that sadly, I was just like King Xerxes (with a significantly lower budget!). I wanted to *prove* that I was a little more righteous, or virtuous, than the person who sent the email to me. I wanted to *earn* the approval of all my social media friends along with their condemnation of the sender. Even if I wrapped words of righteous anger around my actions, my motives were impure.

Have you ever had something to prove or something to earn that resulted in self-centered or self-serving actions? Describe the situation and what happened.

Many times, tainted motives spring from gaps in our lives. These are places that I've come to call holes in our souls. The author of Esther doesn't do any psychoanalysis on the king, but knowing humanity like we do, we can dig out two possible sources for his motives. Sin and flaws are holes in our souls that manifest in a myriad of negative ways.

Sin	Flaws
Pride	Insecurity
Arrogance	People-pleasing
Thinking more highly of ourselves than others	Insecurity
Desire to control	Craving others' approval

Almost certainly, the king had at least one of these holes in his soul and probably many more. So do we. That's why it's essential that we pause before we act to parse our motives. We need to ask ourselves these questions:

1. Am I doing __________ to try to prove something?
2. Am I doing __________ to try to earn something?

If the answer is "yes" to either question, it doesn't mean that we should hide in shame. The need for approval is natural, but the only kind of approval that truly satisfies comes from God.

Not only does He provide satisfaction, He fills the holes in our souls!

It's when we don't turn to God, we end up like King Xerxes, willing to sacrifice anything or anyone to meet his need for affirmation and prowess. When our motives are mixed, we look to others to meet our expectations in inappropriate ways.

Review Esther 1:12. Who was the ultimate recipient of King Xerxes' expectations?

____

____

____

____

How did she respond, and what were the consequences?

____

____

____

____

This is a section of Scripture where I'd love to have more detail! Because I wanted to understand better, I turned to commentaries, books written by biblical scholars that explain the Scripture. Lots of brainy folks have made educated guesses about the motives behind King Xerxes' request and Vashti's response, but none of us know for certain why and how this scene unfolded. I've summarized the scholarly viewpoints below, and you'll see how even their opinions contradict each other.

Conflicting beliefs about King Xerxes' motivations:

- His expectations were appropriate or virtuous because:
  - **He was proud of Vashti and wanted to show her off.** He sent seven eunuchs because he planned for her to enter, carried on a royal platform like the queen she was.
- His expectations were wildly inappropriate or evil because:
  - **He was drunk.** Matthew Henry said, "If he had not been put out of the possession of himself by drinking to excess,

he would not have done such a thing, but would have been angry at anyone that should have mentioned it."[4]

- **He wanted to humiliate Vashti to show his power.** He sent seven eunuchs as the muscle to make her do what he *knew* she wouldn't want to do.

Conflicting beliefs about Vashti's motivations:

→ Her response was appropriate or virtuous because:
- **She was defending her rightful status.** Queens were traditionally introduced at the beginning of banquets and the prostitutes at the end.
- **She was protecting her dignity.** She refused to display herself for a crowd of drunk men.
- **She was maintaining her modesty.** The traditional interpretation found in Jewish teaching was that the King's request for her to appear in her crown was actually a command for her to appear in *only* her crown, naked except for that one sparkly accessory.

→ Her response was wildly inappropriate or evil because:
- **She was a rebellious wife.** Vashti simply didn't submit to her husband.
- **She was a prideful and entitled royal.** As the granddaughter of Nebuchadnezzar, she was too vain to go to her husband when summoned.

Confusing, right? I presented these points of view so that you can seek God and draw your own conclusions about Xerxes' and Vashti's motivations. Personally, I believe that all these conflicting points of view about these two characters say more about the commentators' biases than about the actual interaction (another book for another time). Biases, not facts, often come to the forefront when we try to interpret others' motives.

The King's *response* tells us most of what we need to know about the root of the King's motivations. The only things we know for *certain* is that Vashti didn't come to him, and the king was furious. "But Queen Vashti refused to come at the king's command delivered by the eunuchs. At this the king became enraged, and his anger burned within him" (Esther 1:12 ESV).

When the king became angry, whom did he turn to for advice?

What advice did they give?

What's your response to this action?

How would you describe the advice that King Xerxes received?

One of the means that I've begun to use when examining my motives is the tool I like to call "red-flag feelings." Listed below are red-flag feelings that signal us to slow down, let our emotions settle, examine our motives, and ask for wisdom before we act.

Red-flag Feeling #1:

Burning Anger. Instead of stuffing anger, we can use its appearance as an indicator to look at our feelings. It's an opportunity to slow down, pause our reaction, and evaluate. In the case of my email, I was furious because of the content, but I was also offended that it was sent to me. My anger was an indicator that I needed to take a hard look at my motives.

Red-flag Feeling #2:

Self-righteousness. In Esther 1:15, King Xerxes asked his counselors for advice, and they reacted with over-the-top self-righteousness. In our world, there are people who will always agree with us, fanning the flames of our anger. What we need in moments of anger is someone who will point us straight back to God, away from ourselves. When I had to decide what to do with my post, I turned to my husband, who is loving but not a "yes man." As one who knows the unchanging wisdom of God, not just one who understands the shifting times, he advised me to spend my time praying instead of posting, a pause that allowed my heated emotions to cool.

How could using anger and self-righteousness as red flags—signaling you to pause and examine your motives—help in your relationships?

Whom do you consult when you need to see yourself and your motives clearly? What qualifications do you have for those you consult?

Thankfully, the social media post that I composed in my head never made it onto the internet. The Holy Spirit interrupted the flow from my brain to my fingers! He humbled me by revealing the holes in my soul. The Holy Spirit used my red-flag feelings, good counsel, and Esther 1 to expose my motives and stop me cold.

King Xerxes had self-centered motives, the kind that never serve us well and often harm those around us. Let's use his negative example as a catalyst to begin examining our own motives and making sure that the holes in our souls don't lead us away from God, also.

Pathway Principle

God can refine our motives when we remain humble.

Memorize

Today, fill in the blanks. If you have access to a recording device (maybe one on your phone), then read the verse aloud into it. Listen to it four times while you're reading it.

"For since the __________ of the world God's __________ __________—his eternal __________ and divine __________—have been clearly seen, being __________ from what has been made, so that people are __________ excuse" (Romans 1:20).

Application

If you haven't read the whole book of Esther yet, complete that assignment first.

Optional: If you've read it, write one sentence per chapter to give a summary of the main idea of that chapter.

Day Four: Superheroes and Other Myths: Why People Never Deserve a Pedestal

Trigger Alert: Today's lesson deals with the topic of sexual violence. If you have experienced sexual abuse or violence of any kind, know that I'm praying that this lesson brings comfort. God has a plan for each of His daughters that is never destroyed by what we might have suffered at the hands of others.

I scrolled the news article with growing grief and disbelief. *No, Lord. Please, not another one.* A Christian communicator that I highly esteemed had fallen. His reputation was posthumously exposed, and it was ugly. The rumors of adultery that had floated around for years before his death were proving to be true despite all the protests from within his ministry while he lived.

I was crushed. I had listened to his sermons. I had wondered at his ability to both intellectually and biblically defend the faith. His gifts were aspirational. He was a kind of superhero in my mind. That made the reality of his brokenness so much harder to hear.

My hero's fall points to a truth that is painful to bear. Every single human who has ever lived is a strange and sometimes tragic mix of good and bad. There are no "good guys" who are fully pure in heart. And there are no "bad guys" who are evil through and through. There are only humans, made exquisite in the image of God and terrible in our fallenness. Each one of us is capable of great good when we're walking with God and part of His story. We're also capable of far worse than our most horrifying nightmare. We have the ability to be heroes but never Messiahs; however, in our humanity we often burden our heroes with savior status.

When Lynn and I planned out this study, we decided we couldn't leave week 1 without including the first part of chapter 2 where the "good guys" of this book are introduced. But today, and the rest of this study, comes with a warning label. Esther might not be who you think she is. She is a gorgeous woman whom God used, but she has some not-so-pretty layers, too. Let's take a compassionate but honest look at a woman who's more like us than we might have thought.

Read Esther 2:1–12. Who are the characters that are still here from chapter 1?

____

____

____

____

____

Who are the new characters?

____

____

____

____

____

Four years passed between Esther 1 and Esther 2. Vashti was exiled in the third year of the King's reign, and Esther was made queen in the seventh year. In the middle, Xerxes went to war as planned against the Greeks, but he suffered a crushing defeat instead of the legacy-building victory for which he had schemed and banqueted.[5]

Although there's no mention of his *current* feelings, consider human reactions after defeat and list some of the emotions that the king may have been dealing with at the beginning of chapter 2.

How do humans often behave when they're dealing with these kinds of emotions?

What advice did his personal assistants propose? How might their advice have appealed to him because of his emotional state?

Although I'm an unabashed believer that Scripture holds all that we need, I also realize that I've too-often brushed by the humanity of the people in God's Word. Although we should use the tool of evaluating emotions very carefully, we shouldn't skip it. We never want to misinterpret the truths of Scripture by making them fit human actions, but we *should* aim to interpret human actions with human emotion in mind. Since the author doesn't give us any indication of the thoughts or motives of the people in the story, we'll use this tool today, thinking through the natural feelings that might have been a factor in the actions of each person.

Perhaps with mixed motives of their own, the advisors helped the king put their counsel into action. Commissioners went to every province to collect young, beautiful virgins to be tested by the king and ultimately to become part of his harem. Esther 2:4 tells us that only one would be chosen as queen.

Let's pause here a moment to look more closely and consider the possible emotions of the women who were part of this exercise. As you continue to process these passages, keep these cultural and historical facts in mind:

- The young women who were chosen had to leave home.
- Though the verb "brought" is used in some places, Esther 2:8 says that "Esther also was *taken* to the king's palace." (my emphasis added)
- Each of these virgins would spend a night with the king which delicately implies a not-so-delicate reality—the loss of their virginity.
- After their night with the king, they would either be chosen as Queen or relegated forever to the harem of concubines that the king kept for his pleasure. The concubines were isolated, forbidden to marry, and some historians estimate that Xerxes may have had upward of three hundred women in his harem.
- Polygamy was a cultural way of life, arranged marriage was the accepted system, and teenaged brides were the norm during this time and for many centuries after.

Make a list of the range of emotions that the women who were collected might have felt. Keep in mind that the culture of this time was far different from our modern understanding of human rights and accepted practices. However, that fact doesn't erase human emotional reactions. This might have been considered an honor by some, a prison sentence by others, and traumatic by many.

Now that we've thoroughly introduced the people in the story so far, we're finally ready to meet the main characters whom we love: Mordecai and Esther! Mordecai is a Jew from the tribe of Benjamin, one of the twelve tribes of the nation of Israel. He took guardianship of Esther when her parents died. Verse 7 tells us that Mordecai "had taken her as his own daughter," an expression that is far deeper and more loving than simply giving her the basics of food and shelter.

Bible Nerd Box

If Mordecai was actually taken into captivity by Nebuchadnezzar, he would have been over one hundred years old by this time. Most commentators think that this reference is used to point out that Mordecai was one of the chosen people. His people were taken into exile, thus he was taken into exile. It also establishes him as a recipient of the Covenant promises. The reference to "son of Kish" may be used by the author to show Mordecai's family ties to Saul. The genealogy also indicates that Mordecai wasn't over one hundred.[6]

Some other things we know about Mordecai in 2:1–12 are that he:

- allowed Esther to be part of the King's contest, or at the very least he didn't prevent it.
- forbade Esther from revealing her Jewish identity.
- paced in front of the harem's housing every day to check on Esther.

What do Mordecai's short biography, adoption, and consequent actions potentially tell you about the motivations that drove him? Do you see a list of both positive and negative motives emerging?

As we continue to acquaint ourselves with each person in the book of Esther, we'll see that Mordecai has an admirable strength of character. The facts above, however, reinforce that there's no such thing as a perfect parent, not even Mordecai.

Now let's take a look at our sweet Esther. There are very few details shared about Esther in the introductory verses.

What does Scripture say about Esther in 2:1–12? What doesn't Scripture say?

My heart goes out to Esther at this point. As I've studied, read, and prayed, I've come to see her as an astonishingly-beautiful, young woman who not only endured the tragic loss of her parents but also persevered under the stress of a life-altering contest. Now she carries the heavy responsibility of the crown. She may have come from humble beginnings, but she has become extraordinary.

Historical Note

Esther, the name by which we generally know her, is a Persian version of her name. Her Jewish name was Hadassah, and you might find this in some Bible translations, too.

That's what we know, but let's take a searching look at what's not included. There's no mention of the law, the divine commands that God had given Israel generations before. There's no description of godly resistance to the culture either. The king calls. Mordecai sends. Esther obeys. There is no record of any attempt by Mordecai or Esther to avoid being part of the king's plan.

Also, Esther didn't reveal her racial identity, but maybe she didn't have much to hide. She and Mordecai blended into the pagan culture well at the beginning of this story. If they had been living according to the law of God, eating kosher, praying regularly, and celebrating the festivals, people would have known them as Jews without a word being spoken. There's seemingly no evidence of their faith in God to give them away.

When we read Scripture in its stripped-down, unvarnished glory, we have a much less glamorous girl in front of us than those presented on screens. She's exceptional but definitely not perfect.

Esther is a young woman who is like us in many ways.

She's a girl who's lived through some hard knocks. She blends in with her culture enough that some might consider her lukewarm. But she's still chosen by God. She's still created to be part of His story.

Just. Like. You.

Just. Like. Me.

There *are* heroes in this world beyond the little ones that emerge in costume from a dress-up box or those in Saturday morning cartoons. There are people, like Esther, who do wonderful things.

But even those folks are simply flawed humans who have likely accomplished great good *and* perpetrated terrible cruelty in the stretch of their life's stories. It's true of my fallen preacher man, and we'll see that it's true of Esther, too, as the story goes on. Being honest about the contradictions can make us despair, but it's a place for hope, too. We each have the call to be an imperfect hero, so we need to extend that grace to all around us. When we keep our heroes flat on the ground instead of up on a pedestal, Superhero status rests with God alone.

How does today's study of Esther make you sad?

How does today's study of Esther give you hope?

Pathway Principle

God knows that we are each capable of both great good *and* terrible cruelty.

Memorize

Today, fill in the blanks. Once you're finished, read it aloud once while clapping your hands in rhythm.

"For since the ________________ of the world God's ________________ ______________—his eternal _____________ and divine ___________—have been clearly seen, being _______________from what has been made, so that people are ____________ excuse" (Romans 1:20).

Now try to say it aloud without looking. Don't worry about mistakes. Just use it as an opportunity to see what your brain hasn't "caught" yet. Read the sections aloud that you had trouble with several more times.

Application

If you haven't read the whole book of Esther yet, complete that assignment first.

Optional: If you've read it, make a list of the characters in Esther and give each one a brief description below.

Day Five: The Mystery of Mixed Motives

Our human temptation is to wriggle off the hook. I've wanted to give myself a pass for:

- stupid things I've said.
- the ways I've hurt people.
- considering myself better than others.
- confidences I've broken.
- promises that I haven't kept.

I'm not just being hard on myself. I can also be loving, humble, and a great friend. Being human means that we're all a blend of good, bad, and very ugly.

Being fully honest, think about what you've learned this week about each of these people, and write what you have in common with each of them.

Xerxes

____

____

Vashti

____

____

Mordecai

____

____

Esther

____

____

Most of us can swing between the motives of all four of these folks in a day, but before you get too disheartened, I want to say something revolutionary.

Your motives don't matter as much as you think.

In the case of each of the people we've encountered this week, God worked despite and sometimes through their motives. It puts our presence in His story into proper perspective. Do we matter? Absolutely. Are our good behaviors and pure motives essential to His story? Nope. We can look at this small bite of Esther and see the truth.

God works despite Xerxes' self-centeredness and anger.

God positions His people through Vashti's refusal to comply to her king.

God uses Mordecai even though he's a less-than-perfect parent.

God places Esther in the palace despite her lukewarm faith.

God's providence is immovable despite His people's wavering faithfulness.

In the Old Testament book of Esther, we see God's providence at work as His people wait for the coming Messiah. As commentator Karen Jobes says, "Regardless of whether they always knew what the right choice was or whether they had the best of motives, God was working through even their imperfect decisions and actions to fulfill his perfect purposes."[7]

We dearly love the comfort in quoting Romans 8:28, "And we know that in all things God works for the good of those who love him, who have been called according to his purpose." While we hope for those shining outcomes, we often think that God's good work is blocked by our imperfections. We see in Esther that's simply not true. We've given ourselves too much credit. That's good, good news for us who can get tripped up by our own perfectionism . . . but it's not an excuse.

Do our motives matter at all? Yes! Although pure motives aren't essential to God's work, He desires to make us spotless in every way. God kept His ancient promises to Esther and Mordecai in spite of their shortcomings while they waited for the promised Messiah. In the same way, God works His good in our lives while we wait for the promise of Jesus' second coming. He's always about His redeeming and rescuing work.

Write Romans 8:29 below.

____

____

____

____

What transformational new promise is being made for those who follow Jesus?

____

____

____

____

In what way do you rely on God's promises in the same way that Esther and Mordecai did?

____

____

____

____

The role our motives play in God's story are a bit mysterious in Esther, but we can apply The Clarity Principle by looking at some other passages in the Bible.

Read each of these passages in the New International Version translation of the Bible (if you don't own one, you can find it online). Then draw a line from the Scripture reference to the truth it reveals about motives.

Proverbs 16:2	The Lord will reveal motives at His second coming.
I Corinthians 4:5	Wrong motives can block prayers being answered.
Philippians 1:18	Motives can only be weighed by the Lord.
James 4:3	God can use both false and true motives in preaching.

From these passages, we can see that our motives don't limit God, but they are still relevant. There are three big takeaways that we can apply to our own lives and to our further study of Esther.

Only the Lord Truly Knows People's Motives

This is an important truth to hold as we deal with both ourselves and others. We can guess at people's motives by looking at their actions, just like we've been doing in our study, but we can never be sure of their motives. It's a dangerous judgement to make.

Making assumptions about people's motives has certainly come back to bite me. As most people do, I tend toward attributing bad motives to actions that I don't like. The problem with that is that it damages relationships by creating defensiveness, discounting wounds, or condemning unfairly. Go back to Vashti and think about all the conflicting viewpoints that pastors and theologians have leveled at her, and then answer these questions.

Have you ever had conflicting reports circulating about you? If so, describe the situation.

Why is it dangerous to ascribe motives to others?

Even our own motives can be murky. It's all-too-easy to deceive ourselves, and we'll almost always judge our own motives more gently than the harsh ones we deliver to others. Unless someone comes out and tells us their motives, it's better to leave the judging to God. He's the only One who knows the true weight of every motive, so He's the sole, qualified Judge.

God Can Use Both Good and False Motives for His Purposes

The person doesn't have to be good, and their actions don't have to be godly in order for God to redeem and rescue.

God moves despite mixed motives.

As we've seen in Esther, the New Testament reinforces God's ability to use all things for good. That doesn't mean that all people and all circumstances are good. It simply means that our all-powerful God can redeem them.

Volumes have been written about this mysterious co-mingling of the worlds' evil with God's redemption. It's a hard concept to grapple with, and I almost went under with confusion after my dear friend Linda, the mother of two small sons, died from breast cancer when we were in our early thirties. In the midst of my darkest days after Linda's death, a friend gave me *A Grace Disguised* by Jerry Sittser. It helped me with the complex matter of God using all manners of evil—sickness, abuse, death, etc.—for good.

In *A Grace Disguised*, Sittser recounts the year after a terrible car accident in which a drunk driver killed his mother, wife, and one of their four children. Sittser suffered immeasurable agony over this evil incident, but he also saw God do amazing good in the year that followed. At the end of the book as he processes the seeming contradictions of tragedy and joy, Sittser says, "The badness of the event and the goodness of the results are related, to be sure, but they are not the same. That the latter is a consequence of the former, but the latter does not make the former legitimate or right or good."[8]

Did God's use of King Xerxes make the king's brutal actions good? No. But could God bring good from those terrible actions? Yes. In God's grace and mercy, He is able to redeem our worst sins and our darkest motives. This ability is part of His loving character.

Wrong Motives Do Have Consequences

Although the weight of perfecting our own motives is lifted, that doesn't mean that bad motives don't have consequences. James 4:3 says, "When you ask, you do not receive, because you ask with wrong motives, that you may spend what you get on your pleasures." It's very clear that some prayers are not given a "yes" if we're praying with wrong or self-centered motives. I see the mercy of God even in this! There have been many times that I've prayed for things that in retrospect would have been damaging to me or others. God's always consistent, and His "no" was a rescuing work.

I've seen this truth play out in Lynn's life in real-time. I remember our early conversations about her involvement at Changed Choices, the organization she mentioned in the introduction. It's true that her original motives were mixed. My huge-hearted friend wasn't just thinking about serving others. She was also weighing how to get her book into more hands.

But over time, I've watched our good God use those originally-mixed motives and purify them until they shine like gold. In His wondrous mixture of Providence and Sovereignty, the way He reigns over everything, He's leveraged flawed motives to do a great work in and through Lynn.

She has become a gift to the previously-incarcerated women whom she loves, and they're a treasure to her, too. It's a beautiful thing to see. I've watched God transform motives in my own life, and I'll bet you've seen it in yours, too.

Motives matter, but God moves *despite* mixed motives.

Pathway Principle

God uses us despite our mixed motives.

Memorize

Today, cover our memory verse with your hand and repeat it four times. Peek without shame if you need to!

"For since the creation of the world God's invisible qualities—his eternal power and divine nature—have been clearly seen, being understood from what has been made, so that people are without excuse" (Romans 1:20).

Application

Today's the last call! If you haven't read the whole book of Esther yet, set a reminder on your phone for a time to read it before the next meeting. You'll be glad you did! Even though I've issued lots of warnings this week not to Hollywood-ize the book of Esther, it's got more plot twists than the best movie I've ever seen.

Motives Pathway Principles

God's motives are always pure, so we ask Him to refine ours.

God is faithful and ever-present, even when it seems He's vanished.

God is the author of our story.

God can refine our motives when we remain humble.

God knows that we are each capable of both great good *and* terrible cruelty.

God uses us despite our mixed motives.

Prayer

God, You are faithful and true. Your motives toward Your world and me are good. When I'm in uncertain circumstances beyond my control, I will trust that You are writing my story even when I can't see You. I'm thankful that my mixed motives don't disqualify me from being part of Your story. Please show me where you want to refine me and make me more like You, pure in all my ways. In Jesus' name, Amen.

Questions for Discussion or Personal Journaling

1. Describe how you generally react to uncertainty (i.e., with fear, shutting down, jumping into action, etc.).

2. After completing the study this week, how have your beliefs about the main characters changed? Why have they changed? What is one way that our invisible God has shown Himself to you?

3. What is one new thing you learned directly from the Scripture reading this week?

4. What resonated with you the most this week? How will you apply this idea in your life moving forward?

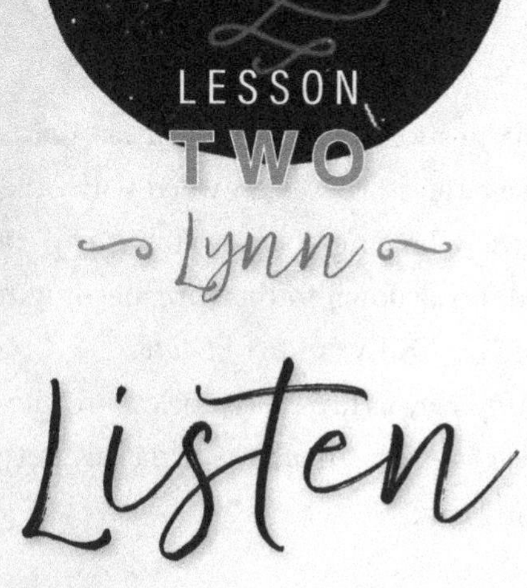

LESSON TWO

Lynn

Listen

Day One: The Winning Combination

Welcome to week 2! It's me, Lynn. I'll be writing this week as we learn about listening from Esther.

Listening has been a huge struggle in my life. Maybe it comes with being the seventh child in a family with eight kids. That's a lot of people wanting talk time.

I could tell you many stories when refusing to listen has gotten me into trouble. (But then I wouldn't be listening!) I won't do *that*, but I will share one.

I should have never been at driving class for . . . speedsters. My lack of listening, actually of reading signs, had gotten me in trouble, again. My second ticket landed me in mandatory classes. Did I mention I wasn't a new driver? I was a mom of *three* teenagers and here I was in speed school!

What a waste of time and $250, pride whispered in my ear.

Instead of listening to the instructor, I chose to write my to-do list, soothing my productive sore spot. Texting my husband Greg, I told him I'd run errand #1 immediately following class. Yes, a check mark on my list was exactly what I needed to turn this day around!

"That's a lot to cram in. Just wait," he responded. *Where was the praise for my effort?*

Ignoring his suggestion, I ran to my car as soon as the doors flung open. Can you believe the store was crowded with other errand-running folks when I arrived? Glancing at my watch every couple of minutes, I waited to be helped. I was down to the wire, needing to pick up our kids soon. Finally, I sped out so I wouldn't be late.

Flopping into my car, I threw my stick shift into reverse when . . . BAM! *Where did that pole come from?* Yes, after just getting out of driving school, I smashed my car.

When has *not* listening been costly or gotten you into trouble?

____

This week, we'll see Esther display the skill of listening as well as the quality of humility, the best place for us to begin if we hope to impact our world.

Read Esther 2:12–14. Record phrases or concepts standing out to you here.

____

Outward beauty has been a thing for us women, each decade and generation changing the rules. Amy and I are both allowing the natural silver to begin shining through our dark heads of hair. I'm not sure about Amy, but there is an underlying part of me that wrestles with it each time I look in the mirror.

Esther's problems are much deeper than what she sees in a mirror.

One night decides where she'll spend the rest of her life: on a queen's throne or in a harem's corner.

I wonder if I were in Esther's position if I would have struggled with sulking? Wrestling with God for allowing me to be in this competition of sorts where I wasn't sure I'd succeed?

Like Esther, God allows you and me to experience situations where we don't know the outcome. Why do you think God would ever allow uncertainty?

Scripture doesn't tell us how Esther felt about this position she was in. Maybe I'm wrong. Perhaps Esther saw this as an opportunity for an upgrade in her life, a chance to be surrounded by lavish extravagance.

While there's little known about her feelings, we can clearly see how she responded.

Before her night with the king, each woman "was given whatever she desired to take with her from the harem to the king's palace" (Esther 2:13 ESV). The wisdom she needed fell on herself. Though she would have only lived in the palace for a year, in a foreign environment, she would need to take what she deemed best.

Bible Nerd Box

The historical pattern was for Persian queens to be chosen from within other noble Persian families, but this king does not follow this norm. These women were gathered from all the provinces of King Xerxes' vast kingdom. "This is what makes it possible for this humble, Jewish woman to have a shot of moving from peasant girl to queen of Persia."[1]

As Esther spent her year in preparation, she would have had time to wonder: *Where is this taking me? Will the king choose a queen before I get my chance? Am I wasting my time? Will I be tossed aside like others before me?*

Scripture speaks to Esther's questions as well as ours: Preparation is never wasted. If we listen and learn with a heart of obedience, we will see the return on our investment.

Preparation is never wasted.

Look up Galatians 6:7. What does God promise?

As His daughters, this is our goal: to be women God uses, pointing others to Jesus. If we have a teachable spirit, intentionally choosing to listen and learn, God will use our experiences for His glory.

As you open your heart and mind to being a woman God uses to help others, what are some ways God has possibly been preparing you?

Read Esther 2:15–18. Under extreme pressure, what does Esther do with her only opportunity, determining her entire future?

Earlier in Esther 2:9, we read how Esther pleased Hegai, winning his favor. Now, Esther wisely turns to him for advice.

Looking for clues in this chapter, what do you think could have brought about this unique relationship between Esther and Hegai?

Logic would tell us Hegai was Persian, knowing cultural differences between king and commoner. Esther understands she doesn't know what she doesn't know. She chooses wisely, to trust Hegai's years of palace experience and possibly his proximity to the king rather than her own intuition.

Proximity will always cause you to gain more knowledge than you could ever obtain from a distance.

Someone once told Bryan Stevenson, lawyer and social justice advocate, "You can't understand most of the important things from a distance. You have to get close." [2]

Maybe the piece that drew Hegai and Esther into their unique relationship was proximity. Being close to people, whether in actual living conditions or in vulnerable relationships, allows us to listen to their stories—what they've been through and what's been done to them. It's the humanity piece.

Both Hegai and Esther experienced pain. Esther had lost her parents. Both Hegai and Esther were in a palace, disconnected from their families. They were both in service to a narcissistic king, who ignored the needs of those around him, not taking into consideration how his actions impacted others. [3]

Could their connection have come from their mutual trauma?

Esther 2:8 told us ". . . Esther also was taken into the king's palace, and put in custody of Hegai." "Taken" and "custody" are the same words used in the English language when referring to prisoners. The same word is used in Esther 2:16: *taken*. These words emphasize Esther had no choice in coming to the palace, unless you count the choice of death. Esther, not unlike some women around the world today, suffered from gender injustice, unable to make her own choices.

"Women in Babylonia like most ancient societies had few rights. A woman's role was in the home and failure to fulfill her duties as a wife was grounds for divorce. A woman who neglected her husband and the house could be drowned. If a woman was found to have committed adultery they could be drowned."[4]

Hegai was a eunuch, a servant or slave who was castrated for the purpose of making him a reliable servant of King Xerxes' royal court. He was maimed, abused, and traumatized.

Bible Nerd Box

"Eunuchs were considered the most suitable guards for the many wives or concubines a ruler might have in his palace, and the eunuchs' confidential position in the harems of princes frequently enabled them to exercise an important influence over their royal masters and even to raise themselves to stations of great trust and power . . . Most eunuchs underwent castration as a condition of their employment, though others were castrated as punishment or after they had been sold by poor parents."[5] While this may have been a normal practice in this time period, that doesn't make it a good practice for the recipients of these acts.

Both Esther and Hegai were broken people. We all are, whether because of choices made for us or made by us.

As we listen to one another and in vulnerability share our mutual brokenness, God can use this brokenness to draw us toward one another. It's an invitation to come alongside, to develop compassion, and to help one another.

What is an area of brokenness in your life God may want to use to help another?

As my stepfather grew older and began losing his hearing, he also became quiet. When he and I chatted in the living room, he would share stories of his childhood and his opinion on all kinds of things, especially politics. But when the room filled with people, his words stopped. He revealed one day why he got so quiet. When it was him and I, talking face to face, he could hear me and read my lips. When the room became noisy and he couldn't see the person talking, he couldn't hear or see their lips. He became silent, not understanding the conversation.

Who are the people in your community who are silent because others are not turning to listen to them? The ones who need someone in close proximity in order for them to speak and become heard?

Look up Matthew 9:36. In the verse prior (v. 35) we see that Jesus is in close proximity to the crowd. What effect did this have on Jesus?

When up close, Jesus showed compassion for people. If I want God to use me to be a part of bringing His love and ways of doing life to earth, I must get close to those who are suffering.

What would it look like for you to get "up close and personal" to those who are suffering?

For me, it is close enough to hear and close enough to read lips, if need be.

Let's get close enough to hear and close enough to read lips.

Listening gave Esther the wisdom she needed—what she needed to please the lustful king and win the throne, but most importantly, to position herself to save her nation, the nation from which the Messiah, Jesus, the Savior of the world, later came.[6]

Pathway Principle

Developing a listening and learning heart makes room for God to use us for His glory and to draw others to Himself.

Memorize

"My dear brothers and sisters, take note of this: Everyone should be quick to listen, slow to speak and slow to become angry" (James 1:19).

Read the memory verse aloud four times. Read it very slowly the first time and faster each subsequent time.

Application

Think of one obstacle keeping you from truly listening to others. How might practicing good listening change your relationships?

Day Two: Listening: Getting on the Preparation Pathway

I had done it again.

Trying to deepen a budding relationship, I invited a friend to a night of worship. When two people are getting to know one another, sometimes there's that dreaded silence. I resorted to my natural response—talking. *Lots and lots of words.* Later on, I reflected on the night. Though we had spent three hours together, I chatted away the majority of the time, wasting the precious opportunity to listen and learn. It was time for change, time for me to become a better listener like Esther.

As a Jewish girl coming into a Persian palace, Esther didn't immediately have the knowledge needed to do the work God had for her. She was a woman operating in an environment that was outside her education and expertise. Listening could help her. Listening to Hegai could expand her knowledge about the king and his ways. Listening to what was happening around her could help her understand how to behave in this place. Listening to God could help her gain the wisdom He promises to those of us who ask (James 1:5). All this listening could help Esther navigate these uncertain circumstances.

Listening gives us tools to move from outsider to insider, the place of true influence.

It was important for Esther to be careful to *whom* she listened. All too often when we are in a hard place, we are tempted to reach out to those who can relate to us, especially those who will agree with what we think. Esther didn't need a voice that would agree with what she thought. She needed the voice who had what she didn't have—a person who might in fact not agree with her ideas at all, but had the knowledge she needed.

Esther had been in the company of Hegai from the time she was taken into the king's palace (Esther 2:8). During this time, she would have been able to observe his character and listen to what he knew about the king. She would have discerned: This is the right one to listen to.

Listening to Hegai and humbling herself before she went to the king allowed Esther to not be humiliated after she went to the king. To be used by God and fulfill His purpose in her, humility had to come first. In this way, she reminds me of Jesus, humbling Himself to fulfill His father's purpose.

Read Philippians 2:3–11. How did Jesus humble Himself?

____

____

____

____

Verses 9–11 tell us the result of Jesus humbling himself. What was it?

____

____

____

____

Jesus Acts on Behalf of the Humble

When Esther humbled herself, asking Hegai for help, he supplied it (Esther 2:15). Over and over again, we see in the gospels, Jesus moves and acts on behalf of those who humble themselves as well.

Look up and read the following passages. Draw a line from the Scripture to Jesus' acts on behalf of those who came to Him.

Matthew 8:1–4	Jesus heals the Centurion's servant.
Mark 5:25–34	Jesus heals the woman with the issue of blood.
Luke 19:1–10	Jesus heals the leper.
Matthew 8:5–12	Jesus goes to Zacchaeus' house.

Jesus listens to one representing the power oppressing God's chosen people, giving him his request. He addresses a woman who's dared to touch Him, healing her. Jesus reaches for a contagious man, restoring him. Calling to the man in a tree, He says, "Take me home with you." Jesus, the One with the name above all names, chose to humble Himself and listen to people.

Want to learn more about Jesus and humility?
See Luke 14:7–11 and Luke 18:9–14.

There is something very humbling about listening. It is admitting my knowledge falls short. It is admitting to others and to ourselves: "I don't know what I need to know. You do. Teach me. Guide me." This is why humility is so hard to embrace. If I humble myself and admit what I don't know but need to know, I'm afraid I'll look weak or unqualified, even overly vulnerable.

Instead, my old self, the part of me resistant to change and being made new by Jesus, wants to "fake it 'til I make it".

Esther didn't hope to "fake it 'til she made it". Nor did she simply ask for advice. Asking for advice leaves the door open to not take the advice given. Esther didn't ask for advice, "she asked for nothing except what Hegai the king's eunuch, who had charge of the women, advised" (Esther 2:15 ESV). Esther didn't just hear what Hegai said; she listened and *did* what Hegai said.

Hearing and listening are not the same thing. According to Dictionary.com, the word *hear* appears to be simply taking in information, whereas *listening* is paying attention with the intention of future action.

You and I may struggle to listen for different reasons. Those of us who wrestle with pride, wanting to be the wisest in the room, don't desire to learn new things from new people. There is the pull to be right.

You may have a hard time listening because you fear being exposed as wrong or bad if you learn you're wrong. We may fear being rejected or thought worthless when our lack of knowledge is revealed. Perhaps listening to others makes us feel inadequate. Maybe we're scared of learning things we didn't know, even scared of being in the know, because then we'll feel obligated to help or "fix" something. What if I'm taken advantage of? Others of us fear the process of listening because what if I listen to another and it's not reciprocated?[7]

Esther left all this behind and laid down her pride.

If we don't humble ourselves, lay down our pride, and choose to be listeners who learn, what does Proverbs 18:12 tell us our future holds?

What does Proverbs 18:12 tell us our future holds *if* we humble ourselves?

Read 1 Peter 5:6 and James 4:6, 10. Who is responsible for doing the humbling?

Last week, Amy mentioned how the name of God is not mentioned in the book of Esther. Also absent in the book of Esther is the mention of prayer, the law or Torah, the commandments God had given His children many years before Esther. There's no mention of central Israelite customs or practices of the temple where they worshipped. The book of Esther never speaks of the promised land God had promised to the Israelite ancestors. Esther doesn't speak of the Israelites who returned to Jerusalem after Nebuchadnezzar of Babylon had taken them captive. There is no mention of the rebuilding of their temple in the city of Jerusalem. (Read more of this particular history of the Israelites in 2 Kings 25:1–21.) And while God reverses things in their favor over and over again, the usual overt miracles or angelic interventions are not there.

Reread Esther 2:15–18 and write down any details that are obviously absent.

One thing that caught my eye is that verse 15 doesn't tell us why Esther was winning favor.

Read Proverbs 3:34. To whom does God give favor?

It takes a great deal of humility for us to realize that every person we come into contact with is made in the image of God and therefore has something to offer to us.

Since most of us would rather be heard than listen to another, I wonder if the other virgins asked Hegai for advice or missed the wealth of wisdom right before them. Why, when wisdom was accessible, would they choose to go their own way instead of asking for help?

Why do I do this myself?

Why do I make decisions with my limited knowledge, strength, and education? Why, when I can access people who have knowledge and wisdom I need? Why, when I have within me the very power of the Holy Spirit, who can give me supernatural wisdom, strength, and divine perspective?

It goes back to a core weakness of mine—yes, the "fake it 'til you make it" part. Can I just tell you that typing this makes me a little sick to my stomach? *Why in the world am I going here?* Because I believe when you and I know our core weaknesses, we're more aware of our enemy's particular schemes against us (Job 1:7; 1 Peter 5:8).

Knowing our core weaknesses can cause us to be more aware of the enemy's particular schemes against us.

So, what does this have to do with listening?

If our core desire is to be respected, admired, successful, or valuable, isn't that compromised when I admit that I don't know something? Yes, it is . . . and that is exactly why God wants us to humble ourselves. Humbling myself gives pride a death blow.

Back to Proverbs 18:12. What needs to come first?

More humility!

Humbling ourselves and seeking God's knowledge is His idea. As Proverbs 18:15 tells us, "An intelligent heart acquires knowledge, and the ear of the wise seeks knowledge" (ESV).

What steps, then, can we take to humble ourselves? (Warning: We are heading into waters for those serious about becoming mature in Christ!)

Bible Nerd Box

Want to learn more about how God sees pride? Check out Psalm 10:4; Proverbs 8:13; and Proverbs 16:18–19.

A key first move for me is repenting of pride. Pride, a roadblock to listening, keeps me from admitting, to both others and to myself, what I need to know and what I don't know.

In her Bible study, *Surrendered*, Barb Roose calls out the truth, "Any one of us can fall into the trap of self-promotion or pride, whether it's wanting to be praised for leading a particular ministry, using a gift that's publicly recognized . . . we're all susceptible to using for our own gain what others should see as God's glory."[8]

What warning does Proverbs 11:2 give us if we choose not to humble ourselves?

____

____

____

How did Esther experience the working out of Proverbs 11:2 here in Esther 2?

____

____

____

As we humble ourselves, listening begins to alleviate the pain of not knowing what we need to know. It's like the psoriasis on my skin. When exposed to the sun, healing begins. If I cover it up, it's itchy, red, and irritated. Seeing my skin sores is uncomfortable. I'd rather hide them, especially from others.

But exposure brings what is needed. Esther's own exposure of her lack brought her what she needed.

So, it is when we expose what needs the Son's light in our lives. We come before Father, take pride out of hiding, and ask Him to forgive our sin. Gently and with love, Father forgives and sets us free from ourselves and there, in freedom, we can be used by Him. As we humble ourselves to learn from both Father and others, we begin to see our helplessness, guilt, shame, fear, embarrassment, and worthlessness fall off. We're moving deeper into the waters of preparation to be used by God.

Pathway Principle

Listening requires humility.

Memorize

Today, write out the memory verse four times and then read all four times aloud. Circle words that are meaningful to you.

"My dear brothers and sisters, take note of this: Everyone should be quick to ________, slow to _________ and slow to become angry" (James 1:19).

Application

As you pray, ask the Lord to show you one person to listen to and learn from. Then, reach out to him or her today.

Day Three: Listen In

Following yesterday's application, I reached out to one person to listen to and learn from. Stephanie was the pre-release manager for Changed Choices, an organization I volunteer with which empowers women building new lives after prison walls. I knew little about mass incarceration and the reason it exists today. I was hoping Stephanie could teach me more about the work needing to be done to bring change.

When we sat down for coffee, I didn't feel anxious. The more we chatted, though, the more nervous I became as it became apparent how little I knew. At one point, in her wisdom, Stephanie said, "This is a long, slow work that many before you have been doing for many, many years." She was right. I was a newbie and had much to learn.

Esther recognized Hegai knew much more than she did in the area she was moving into and you and I need to do the same. God has already called women and men of God to go before us in bringing His kingdom—His love, salvation, and ways—to the earth.

Read 1 Peter 5:5–6. What action does Peter call us to take?

Listening to Other People in Order to Love

In addition to listening to those who know more, we also need to listen to those who need our Father's love. Listen in order to give them what they need.

What is the first action listed in James 1:19?

I really like reading verses in a variety of translations and paraphrases to bring new insight; it is another tool I use when studying the Bible. Look at how The Message paraphrase translation reads James 1:19: "Post this at all the intersections, dear friends: Lead with your ears, follow up with your tongue, and let anger straggle along in the rear" (MSG).

Lead with your ears—now that is great advice! My husband often quotes a friend with more good advice, "Listen with your eyes." There is so much we can learn when we are quiet and listen.

In his book, *The Listening Life*, Adam S. McHugh tells us we often listen the wrong way: "Trying to fix, judge, rescue or change others are all subtle ways of exerting power over other people. Instead of entering into the world of another person, we try to force them to enter ours . . ." Adam helps to remind us people are not one-dimensional; they are ". . . complex, layered, multifaceted, beautiful, wounded, contradictory, beloved image-bearers of the Creator. They are minds, hearts, souls, and bodies, spilling over with dreams, passions, hurts, and fears."[9]

Remember on day 2 when I talked about the evening out with my new friend? The next time we got together, I tried to be quiet and allow silence to fill the space so she could talk. I tried to listen, to enter her world. Do you know how it felt? Uncomfortable! But how was she ever going to share if I kept filling all the space with my words? The more time I made for her to speak and the more time we allowed for trust to grow, the more she began to share.

If you are like me and struggle to listen, ask yourself this question: What might I miss if I'm not listening?

____

____

____

____

____

____

> **"Many people are looking for an ear that will listen. They do not find it among Christians, because the Christians are talking when they should be listening."[10] (Dietrich Bonhoeffer)**

In our efforts to become better listeners, we can begin asking ourselves about our conversations:

- Am I currently thinking of what I will say next?
- Is my mind on a different topic entirely, maybe even making a list of things I need to do?
- Am I doing something while the person is talking? (Unloading the dishwasher, cooking a meal, folding laundry, checking my phone, driving?) Am I communicating that they are not as important as what I am doing?
- As they share, am I thinking of what they've done wrong or how their thinking is "incorrect"?
- What is my motivation for listening? Is it to love them better?
- Am I asking too many questions?

That last one might throw you off a bit. Questions can be a way of learning more about another, but it can also be a way of getting information I want or being in control.[11] I have even caught myself listening, collecting ammunition to use in the future. Ever been there?

When we don't listen for the sake of understanding, we become like King Xerxes in Esther. Instead of seeking to understand Vashti, he pushed his way, attempting to gain respect through his decree rather than earning it through honorable actions.

To learn how listening begins with seeing, dig into Acts 3:1–10.

Listening to Culture

Read Esther 2:19–23. I was under the impression Esther's move from a normal Jewish girl to a queen who changes her world went relatively fast. (As a get-er-done kind of gal, that tends to be my pattern—fast.) Yet that's not the story. First, she had twelve months of preparation. Once chosen, life seems relatively quiet over the next five years.

 **Read Esther 2:16 and 3:7 below.**

> "She was taken to King Xerxes in the royal residence in the tenth month, the month of Tebeth, in the seventh year of his reign" (Esther 2:16).
>
> "In the twelfth year of King Xerxes, in the first month, the month of Nisan, the *pur* (that is, the lot) was cast in the presence of Haman to select a day and month. And the lot fell on the twelfth month, the month of Adar" (Esther 3:7).

I'm sure during this time Esther was continuing to learn more about her new role as well as more about the lifestyle, expectations, religions, and traditions of the Persians.

In Esther 2:19, we meet up with Mordecai. "When the virgins were assembled a second time, Mordecai was sitting at the king's gate." This phrase [sitting at the king's gate] refers to holding an official position in the court. The gate entering into the walled palace complex was a large building in which legal, civil, and commercial business was transacted."[12]

Mordecai was not just sitting, filling a position in his community. Mordecai was listening. He was aware of what was happening around him, in his culture (Esther 2:19, 21). When he hears of a plot detrimental to the king, he speaks up to Esther and she listens (Esther 2:22).

As a woman with privilege, Esther didn't need to be informed of what was happening outside her palace. She had her king, her house, her chariot. She could have just enjoyed her life.

That's what I'm tempted to do—not listen outside my four walls.

I want to shelter myself because I don't want to hurt. I try to avoid the news and not read posts that might make me sad.

Esther chose to listen to Mordecai. She paid attention and listened to what was happening in her community and culture. When the plot was found to be true, the king's life was saved (Esther 2:22–23). The score so far: *Esther 1–Evil 0.*

Esther practiced a life of listening. Listening to Mordecai allowed Esther to play a key role in saving the king's life. As his queen, with the revelation of this attempted coup, she would have been saving her own life as well. Esther proves to the king that she is not just a pretty face on his arm, but a wise woman to whom he is now indebted for his very life.

Pathway Principle

Lead with your ears.

Memorize

Today, fill in the blanks. If you have access to a recording device (maybe one on your phone), read the verse aloud into it. Then listen to it four times while you're reading it.

"My dear ______ and ________, take note of this: Everyone should be quick to ______, slow to ________ and slow to become ______" (James 1:19).

Application

What steps can you take to listen and learn in your community? I'll give you a couple for starters: YouTube videos and following ministries with similar passions.

Be sure to listen to a variety of voices. When we only listen to those who believe exactly like us or have opinions that coincide with our own, that is called an echo chamber.[13] In this environment, our learning is limited because only our existing view is reinforced, and alternative ideas are not considered.

Day Four: Our History with Listening

Esther 2 wraps up with the results of Esther's revelation of the assassination plot to kill the king: "And when the report was investigated and found to be true, the two officials were impaled on poles. All this was recorded in the book of the annals in the presence of the king" (Esther 2:23). We're not told of any promotion given to Mordecai for the good he had done by disclosing the deadly information, but we are introduced to a new character, promoted with no reason given.

Read Esther 3 and note below anything you are wondering about or that is not obviously revealed.

____

____

____

____

As we've been reading through Esther, we see an absence of many details. Sometimes I think God purposely leaves out details in Scripture so we don't think there's a formula. We really love those 1, 2, 3 steps—at least I do. Give me a good list and I'm ready to go.

As chapter 3 unfolds, we see for the first-time potential tension between the Jews and the Gentiles. The king has again demanded honor be given (flashback to Esther 1 when another demand for honor was made). This time the king commanded all to bow down and pay Haman homage (Esther 3:2).

Mordecai refuses to do so (Esther 3:2).

There is no clarity given for Mordecai's reason for not bowing down. It seems to be implied that he refused to bow because he is a Jew, but that's not clear. Historians have noted that Jews did bow to pagan officials following court protocol, similar to how you and I would curtsy before the British queen or king if we were to meet them.[14]

What *is* clear is how deeply Mordecai's disrespect is digging into Haman.

As we read this chapter, we again see exaggeration beginning with Haman's reaction to Mordecai. Why would this pride-filled man take his anger for one and apply it to an entire nation?

When the Bible gives us details, they are often clues to deeper meanings. Because you and I don't live in fourth-century BC and most of us wouldn't be well versed in Persian or Jewish culture, many of these details are lost to us. This is just one of many reasons using Bible commentaries when studying God's Word can be so helpful. (See Bible Study Tools Quick Reference in the back of this book.)

The description of Haman's lineage is one such detail that I learned about after consulting various commentaries. Haman is introduced as Haman, the Agagite. When Mordecai was introduced in Esther 2:5, he was called a Benjaminite. What these two descriptions would have told the Jewish reader is there is bad blood between these two officials.

Haman's ancestors were from a heathen nation, a nation who did not recognize the God of the Bible, called Amalek. They were the first people to try to destroy God's people, the Israelites (Exodus 17:8–16). Because of this, God said ". . . I will completely blot out the name of Amalek from under heaven" (Exodus 17:14).

In Deuteronomy 25:17–19, God commanded Israel to finish the job with the Amalekites, blotting out their memory forever. (Aren't you so glad for Jesus' blood today, forgiving us for the times we've gone against God and we experience grace we don't deserve?)

The Israelites didn't accomplish the task of wiping out the Amalekites. Many years later in 1 Samuel 15, the prophet Samuel went to Saul, to both anoint him as king and to give him clear instructions on taking out *all* of Amalek (1 Samuel 15:3).

What does 1 Samuel 15:9 say Saul and the people actually did?

Since they did not obey God, the battle between these two peoples continued.

I remember as a child being amazed at a House of Mirrors. Looking into the mirror in front of me, it appeared as though the mirrors went on and on and on into infinity. In reality, it was the mirror behind me producing this effect.

While it was a fun experience as a child, it is far from fun when a similar effect takes place in the lives of generations as a result of one generation's disobedience. If the Jewish people had fully obeyed God the first time or even the second time, they would have never been in the position they found themselves in Esther.

Disobedience has the power to impact generation after generation. We may think we are making choices that are minor. Even feel that because we obeyed God partially, like Saul, we obeyed God enough. But if we could hold up a mirror, even years past our lifetimes, chances are we would still see the effects of our sin and the sins of those before us (Exodus 34:7).

Again, I am so very thankful for the hope we have in Jesus. Because of His death on the cross, He forgives us when we confess our sins. Through this forgiveness, we can ask for and believe that God will reverse the effects that generations of sin have created.

You may want to take a moment now, to reflect on your family's history. If needed, ask Jesus to forgive sins in the generations before and set your family free of the effects of these sins in the future.

Haman as an Agagite was an enemy of the Jews because of his ancestor's prior history. Thus, when he created a plot to pay Mordecai back for disrespecting him, it wasn't directed at Mordecai alone, but toward all the Jews.

When I read the Bible, one way that I study it is by asking questions—lots and lots of questions. So here, I asked: How would Haman have known this history?

Had the story of the Israelites coming into Amalek and taking it over been written down from their point of view and handed down from generation to generation? Or was it more informal, a story told over and over again, the bitterness building as it was passed on from parent to child? Maybe it wasn't either of these, but more of a passive putting down with attitudes and actions with no real understanding of why or where this prejudice came from?

These are the ways enmity can be passed down, growing in strength from one generation to another. And like Haman the Agagite (Agag was the king of the Amalekites) and Mordecai the Jew, many years later the underlying opposition ranges from unfriendliness to animosity.

In light of this history between Agagites and Jews, how does history between nations and within nations impact how we think of people today?

What if Haman had followed the One True God, humbled himself, asked for forgiveness for the deeds of his ancestors, and asked the same of Mordecai? Might they have been able to listen to one another, possibly understand their past histories, and working in the same kingdom, come to a place of mutual respect, even if their beliefs continued to differ?

While it would not appear from the text that Haman did follow Yahweh, listening should be one of the demarcations of God's children, those who represent the King. We can listen for understanding instead of listening so we can prove we are right. I have seen in my life that when I listen to understand rather than listen to gain evidence for why I'm correct, I learn what I do not know. Opportunity opens to continue and deepen relationships. This is the place where we can foster connections to both introduce another to our King and to give glory to our King.

Pushing to prove instead of listening for understanding severs relationships, causing me to no longer be in a position to share or glorify Jesus.

Pathway Principle

As His children, we are called to listen as a demarcation of being His.

Memorize

Today, fill in the blanks. Once you're finished, read it aloud once while clapping your hands in rhythm.

"My dear ______ ____ _______, take note of this: Everyone should be ____ ___ ______, ________ ___ _________ and ________ ___ _____ ________" (James 1:19).

Hint: you'll use the word *slow* two times.

Now try to say it aloud without looking. Don't worry about mistakes. Just use it as an opportunity to see what your brain hasn't "caught" yet. Read the sections aloud that you had trouble with several more times.

Application

As you think about your personal and family history, is there any story like that of Haman and Mordecai that has influenced your view of people? How does it affect the way that you listen to those people or groups?

Day Five: Is That You You're Listening To?

My ears perked up when a Christian leader on a podcast began to talk about those who write. The host spoke harsh judgements toward those lacking in education and experience. Before I realized it, my brain began spinning in agreement with the host's opinion. I found myself thinking, *Lynn, you have no business writing about God's Word. You have no formal education in the Bible.* I began to relive the times I had been asked about my education, or lack thereof, and the doubt it had raised in my mind before. My heart was flirting with doubt, and I found myself thinking of which path to take next.

Let's begin our day together by rereading Esther 3:6.

What exaggerated desire did Haman have after his encounter with Mordecai?

Haman's excessive anger and desire for violence clues us in to deeper damage in his inner being. Was Mordecai's standing in the city gate a reminder of what he didn't want to face? Did he believe he didn't deserve the respect the king commanded? Does this explosive enmity reveal a deep insecurity that he wasn't who the king made him out to be?

As I've gotten older, I've come to see often what appears to be pride is really the opposite. Lack of confidence, assurance, and self-doubt are shrouded by a curtain, covering up my lack of knowing who I am because of Christ. This was the reason I wrote *Fearless Women of the Bible*, because I needed to find unshakable confidence in my unshakable God. There have been times when my lack of formal education has tried to dismantle the confidence I have in Christ—holding me back from fulfilling what God has called me to. I needed to find confidence in Christ alone; not a confidence built on someone, someplace or something, all things we can lose. I needed to find confidence in the One we can never lose.

If Haman's confidence is built on himself, Mordecai's actions would cause that confidence, when under review, to quake. He knows from seeing or hearing of the king's past volatile actions just how quickly someone can be removed from the king's court . . . or worse. "In those days, while Mordecai was sitting at the king's gate, Bigthan and Teresh, two of the king's officials from those who guarded the door, became angry and sought to lay hands on King Ahasuerus. But the plot became known to Mordecai and he told Queen Esther, and Esther informed the king in Mordecai's name. Now when the plot was investigated and found *to be so*, they were both hanged on a gallows; and it was written in the Book of the Chronicles in the king's presence" (Esther 2:21–23 NASB).

Anytime we are elevated, if the basis of that promotion is not to please King Jesus, we, too, will quiver when we are questioned.

God never created us to stand on the stage of admiration; we were created to give Him adoration.

When *we* are lifted up, instead of lifting *Him* up, that higher ground will heighten every insecurity hidden in our hearts. Insecurity reveals where our confidence lies. Like Haman, is our confidence, our security, in ourselves, our abilities and achievements? If so, when it is called into question, what poured out of Haman will pour out of us, for fear is a powerful fuel. Anger, defensiveness, strife, name-calling, bitterness, gossip—there is no end to the behavior insecurity will birth in us and project onto people.

This was the place where Mordecai found himself, subjected to the effects of Haman shaking in his own skin. I hope neither of us ever experiences the volcanic anger Haman hurled toward God's people. Chances are, though, we're both familiar with the simmer. Someone wrongs us, and we make it much more. It's no longer about the empty gas tank, the money spent, or the job not done. It's about the million little hurts stockpiling in our heart. Maybe even pain that has nothing to do with the person in front of us. And now, this one is about to pay for each and every time we were forgotten, disrespected, or hurt. In reality, it has very little to do with the current offense, and everything to do with what is stored up in our hearts.

Unhealed insecurity can lead to unreasonable reactions when hurt is just below the surface.

Unhealed insecurity can lead to unreasonable reactions when hurt is far below the surface. But just like it could be with Haman, it's not about what just happened. It's about the simmer. Over time, little hurts have been allowed to remain in our heart, where they have been restrained, just below the boiling point. At some time, unless they are dealt with, repented of and healed, they will gush out.

To determine when Haman's anger will pour out on the entire nation of Israel, they "cast Pur (that is, they cast lots)" (Esther 3:7 ESV).

Purim are clay cubes engraved with characters or dots, somewhat like dice. They were used for telling the future, by both the pagans and the Jews alike (Joshua 18:6). Haman began casting the lot during the first month, Nisan, which is the month that the Jews celebrate Passover. How ironic that word of their future destruction is sent out just as the people would be celebrating God liberating them from Egypt many years before (Exodus 12:18; Leviticus 23:5; Numbers 28:16). Later we'll see that this death sentence, for the Persians to attack all Jewish families, is set to occur eleven months later on the eve of Passover itself.

Can you see God setting up His salvation once again, just as He did the children of Israel from Egypt and Pharaoh? Even while evil is plotted against them, God's greater plan is quietly unfolding.

> **"I make known the end from the beginning, from ancient times, what is still to come. I say, 'My purpose will stand, and I will do all that I please'" (Isaiah 46:10).**

How does seeing this set up give you hope for a difficult situation in your life?

____

____

____

____

____

Haman then moved to express his own bias, his feelings and opinion about Jewish people to the king. At this point, King Xerxes appears to be neutral in his feelings toward the Jews. Haman's powerful, but negative, words construct disdain for "a certain people" in the king's heart. Ironically, unbeknownst to the king or Haman, the woman the king loved was one of those people! Specifically, Haman says, "There is a certain people . . . [who] do not obey the king's laws" (Esther 3:8). Haman uses exaggeration for manipulation.

According to the details we have been given so far in the book of Esther, how many of "the certain people" did not obey the king's laws?

If you're seeing what I'm seeing, there was *one* man disobeying *one* law, Mordecai. Haman crafts words to get what he wants: "If it pleases the king . . ." (Esther 3:9). Haman's devious words do their work on the king's mind and heart.

King Xerxes didn't investigate Haman's words. He just listened to the one close to him—the one who had just offered to give him approximately three hundred tons of silver to refill the royal treasury, the bank recently emptied by his disastrous defeat in war, trying to overtake Greece.[15]

In the very next verse, the king takes action, without even knowing who are the people that "do not obey the king's laws" (Esther 3:8).

This king is quite the double-minded man, highly influenced by those to whom he listens, whether for good or bad. Only hearing the coins jingling in his coffers, King Xerxes lacked discernment to recognize he was listening to evil. Indifference is very dangerous as shown with Haman's poisonous prejudice slithering down into the king's heart.

After Haman's powerful speech, the king gives his signet ring to Haman—a sign that Haman is like a son, holding the power of the king (Genesis 41:42). He goes on to give Haman power to do ". . . as it seems good to you" (Esther 3:11 ESV). Because of Haman's bias, what seems good to this man is far from good.

Whether we realize it or not, we are all influenced by what we listen to.

Fill in the chart below of things you listen to in a week. Make a note of whether this is a positive or negative influence in your life. I'll go first.

Action	Influence
My pastor's sermons	Positive
Watching too many newscasts	Negative
____________________	__________
____________________	__________
____________________	__________
____________________	__________

Our world has many words and few filters. Whether through conversation, TV, or social media, we need to be discerning of what we allow to fill our ears and influence our hearts. Evil can creep in subtly and before we know it, we have the same response in our minds: *Whatever seems good* we allow to transform us.

What seemed good to Haman was a law that would have permanent, detrimental repercussions on this group of exiles: ". . . to destroy, to kill, and to annihilate all Jews, young and old, women and children, in one day . . . and to plunder their goods" (Esther 3:13 ESV).

Think of the people you've listened to and how they have impacted the way you view your faith, your community, and your culture. Then complete the section below.

Who	How
Faith:	____________________
Community:	____________________
Culture:	____________________

When the decree was finalized, ". . . the king and Haman sat down to drink, but the city of Susa was thrown into confusion" (Esther 3:15 ESV). Haman and the king with cool callousness celebrate the decision made while those under their authority cycle through confusion. As Proverbs

29:2 says, "When the righteous are in authority, the people rejoice; but when a wicked *man* rules, the people groan" (NKJV).

In what way do you think our culture is thrown into confusion today? From where is the confusion coming? From what is it born?

Let's reflect on all the listening we have seen in these two chapters:

- Esther listened to Hegai (Esther 2:15).
- Esther listened to Mordecai (Esther 2:20).
- Mordecai listened to the conversation at the gate (Esther 2:22).
- Esther listened to Mordecai again (Esther 2:22).
- The king listened to Esther (Esther 2:23).
- The king's servants at the gate listened to the king's command (Esther 3:2).
- Haman listened to the king's servants (Esther 3:4).
- Haman listened to his fury (Esther 3:5).
- Haman listened to the king's servants (Esther 3:6).
- King Xerxes listened to Haman (Esther 3:10, 11).
- The scribes and couriers listened to the king (Esther 3:12–15).
- The people of Susa listened to the king's edict (Esther 3:15).

Just like all of these characters, you and I also do a lot of listening. May we, like Esther, learn to whom to listen and how to listen well.

Pathway Principle

To whom and to what we listen has a profound impact on our lives.

Memorize

Today, fill in the blanks. If you have access to a recording device (maybe one on your phone), read the verse aloud into it. Then listen to it four times while you're reading it.

"My dear ______ ____ _______, take note of this: Everyone should be ____ __ _______, ________ __ _________ and ________ ___ _____ _______" (James 1:19).

Hint: you'll use the word *slow* two times.

Application

Today, be very aware of to whom and to what you are listening. How is all of this listening impacting your life?

Listen Pathway Principles

Developing a listening and learning heart makes room for God to use us for His glory and to draw others to Himself.

> Listening requires humility.
> Lead with your ears.

As His children, we are called to listen as a demarcation of being His.

To whom and to what we listen has a profound impact on our lives.

Prayer

Father, all people are important and deeply loved by You. You are calling me to listen and look out. Look out of my window and into my neighborhood, my community, my city, my country. Look outside of my calendar. Open my eyes to what I'm missing. Move me past projects where I can check a box; Help me see hurting, broken people. People at risk like the king was when his life was threatened. Help me to listen and see people desperate for You and the new life and love You have to give them. Open my eyes to see what words and people have influenced me, both for good and for evil. Help me to hear You. Do true work in my heart. In Jesus' name, Amen.

Questions for Discussion or Personal Journaling

1. When in a group of people, would you say you are more of the talker or the listener in a group? Are there any life experiences that may have contributed to you being more of a talker or listener?

2. Like Esther, God allows you and me times of incredible uncertainty. Why do you think God allows this to happen?

3. Read Proverbs 11:2. Why do you think listening requires humility?

4. As you open your heart and mind to being a woman God created to help others, what are some ways God has possibly been preparing you?

5. What resonated with you the most this week? How will you apply this idea in your life moving forward?

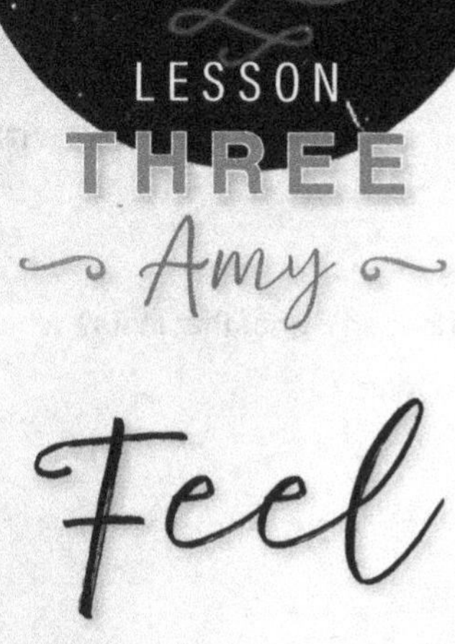

Feel

It's Amy here this week! I ended the week on motives by reminding us that our motives matter, but they don't limit God. Get ready to dive into another hard but good topic with me . . . feelings.

Day One: Feel Good Grief

The cheery cupcake caterpillar stood in sharp contrast to the grief that gripped me. My friend Linda was throwing one of the no-holds-barred birthday parties for which she was famous. She was also valiantly facing her last days with cancer. I giggled along with the children partying around me, but I wanted to put my head down and weep.

When I saw Linda heading for the kitchen to grab more food for the ravaged buffet, I followed to plead with her. "Linda, you look so tired. Please, please sit down a minute and rest."

With a gentle gesture, she laid her hand on my arm. "Amy, this may be the last birthday party that I throw for my son. I truly appreciate your concern, but I'm *not* resting."

That poignant memory is over twenty years old now, but I'm crying even as I type it. There are some losses that never lose their sting. Death ushers in an uncertainty like none other, and there are some hurts that hold on forever. But these are the griefs that can point us straight to the heart of God, connecting us with Him in a way that nothing else does.

When have you experienced a grief that lasts? What memory of a long-ago hurt still brings you to tears?

Go back and reread Esther 3:13–15. Write out the king's edict in your own words. What was the command?

Based on their actions, how would you describe the emotions of Xerxes and Haman concerning the edict?

What was the emotion/reaction of everyone else in the city of Susa to the king's edict?

Despite the fact that Haman and the King had just ordered a horrifying genocide, their actions make us think that they didn't care at all. Evidently, ordering a whole people group killed was just another day at the office for King Xerxes.

While the king and Haman drank (again), expressing a shocking nonchalance, the rest of the populace responded with confusion and bewilderment. These citizens were the ones who were going to have to kill their neighbors after all. "Why?" must have been the all-consuming question.

Read Esther 4:1–3. List the reactions of Mordecai and the Jews to the news of the king's edict.

____

____

____

____

____

Which reactions or emotions that you recorded describe the way you would have reacted if you were a Jew in this setting? Why?

____

____

____

____

____

The average citizen questioned, but the Jews *grieved.* Not only were they facing their own deaths, but they were contemplating the end of God's chosen people. The final blow to His promises. The severed chain of generations that was supposed to lead to a Messiah. In despair, they must have wondered where God was. He had sent them into the discipline of exile, and He had seemingly vanished. They must have worried, "Has He given up on us?"

Have you ever been in a circumstance that rocked you to your core? That made you wonder where God was? Describe it here.

God Grieves, Too

After Linda lost her battle with cancer, leaving her devastated husband, Don, and two tiny boys without a wife or mother, I wrestled with God. How could He allow a beautiful woman who loved Him deeply to die? Where was He in her last moments when she left the family that needed her so much?

In His overwhelming kindness, God sent a surprising and humbling response to my questions. Don showed up at my door one day with a book in his hands. "Amy, I know you must be struggling, so I wanted to bring a resource that sustained me after my first wife died. There are lots of truths in here that comforted me, and I think they'll help you, too."

Yes, Linda was Don's *second* wife to die before he got out of his forties. God sent this man who had faced repeated loss to minister to me. I was a mess, but God reached out in love to me through a grieving husband.

In the book Don brought me, *Where Is God When It Hurts?*, Philip Yancey answers the question that we can have during uncertain times when we're experiencing grief or facing a crisis. He points to the perfect human life of Jesus and His excruciating death saying, "By not making himself exempt, but by deliberately taking on the worst the world has to offer, he gives us the hope that God can likewise transform the suffering each of us must face. Because of his death and resurrection, we can confidently assume that no trial—illness, divorce, unemployment, bankruptcy, grief—extends beyond the range of his transforming power."[1]

As people who live in the grace that Jesus provides through His death, the gifts of forgiveness, freedom, and presence that fulfills the Law, we can look back at the before-the-cross people in Esther and answer the question that must have made their hearts throb. Where is God when it hurts?

He's *with* us, grieving alongside us. Before His redeeming work is revealed, Jesus is present and His tears fall with ours. Does that sound like a stretch?

Read John 11:1–44. Summarize this story in three or fewer sentences.

What was Jesus' response in verse 33?

Why do you think He responded that way when He knew that Lazarus would be raised from the dead?

Jesus' tears have evoked the opinions of many scholars. Despite the debate, I believe that this is a place where we can apply the idea that the simplest and most obvious answer is often the truest one. The simplest answer to why Jesus wept over Lazarus' death is that the grief of those He loved was the trigger for His own flood of sorrow. He joined his tears with His friends'. This is a precious glimpse into the heart of our God.

When we grieve, He grieves, too, because He loves us. How He must have grieved with His people under the threat of the king's evil edict! He knew that redemption was coming, but His tears mingled with theirs in the terror of the moment.

What thoughts and feelings are sparked in you because of knowing that God grieves with you?

How might knowing that God grieves with you allow you to give grief its full expression, even some of the physical ones described in Esther 4:1–3?

Read the Scriptures below and record some of the sources of God's grief.

Ezekiel 6:8–9

Luke 19:41–44

Ephesians 4:30

Did you notice that all three parts of the Trinity—the Father, the Son, and the Holy Spirit—display an expression of heartbreak in the Bible? These are just a few of the Scriptural examples of God's grief. He grieves over humanity's sin, idolatry, rebellion, and rejection. Jesus wept in anguish over His imminent, unjust death. The Holy Spirit is grieved over our sin and rejection. God grieves, so it's good for us, those made in His image, to grieve as well.

As Christians, we've often formed a wonky, mistrustful relationship with our emotions, but it doesn't have to be that way. If we acknowledge our emotions, allowing them to fulfill the purpose for which they were given, our hearts are joined with God's. We lean into grief so we can understand what grieves God.

When we're in pain, we need to remember this truth:

Pain points to a problem.

It might be the problem of death and sickness, a consequence of man's broken relationship with God. Or it could be grievous injustice rooted in the lack of honor for the image of God in each person. That's what the Jews in Persia were facing.

God loves His chosen people, the Jews. What other people groups does He love, care for, and defend?

Psalm 147:3 ______________________________

Amos 5:10–12 ______________________________

Zechariah 7:9–10 ______________________________

God grieves over all that's broken and lost. Scripture tells us He cares for the broken hearted, the poor, the righteous, widows, orphans, and immigrants. Although many of these categories have been politicized, these are people, not just headlines or political pawns. They're people God loves. He's always working to redeem their circumstances, so we don't have to be afraid of joining His team. When we feel sorrow over the conditions and circumstances that grieve Him, it pleases Him.

When we engage our emotions to care for the people that God cares for, we're aligning ourselves with God Himself.

When a Few Tears Aren't Enough

In my white, southern culture, people expect grief to be contained and "appropriate," but sometimes even a whole box of Kleenex isn't enough for the flood of tears. Other cultures show us examples of grief that may be far healthier. For example, tribal African women keen in their grief, rock their bodies and wail. In New Orleans, Dixieland jazz follows funeral processions in an exuberant and intense celebration of life. Some Chinese societies observe one hundred days of mourning, eschewing the belief that we should "move on" quickly.

Mordecai displays his emotions publicly and loudly. I'm sure that if I would have been a Jew living in Persia, I would have been decked out in sackcloth sitting in ashes with all the rest. Adorning themselves this way was an external cultural expression of deep internal grief. It was exhibited by many in Jewish culture. Joshua tore his clothes after a defeat in battle (Joshua 7:6). King David rent his clothing after the death of Saul and Jonathon (2 Samuel 1:11 KJV). After hearing the Torah for the first time, King Josiah ripped his clothes over his own sin and those of the people (2 Kings 22:11 MSG). That expression of grief may seem strange to us, but it's an indication they knew God could handle their strongest emotions. After experiencing God's faithfulness for generations, the Jews knew the One who would hear their cry.

Bible Nerd Box

Daniel 9:3 tells us that dressing in sackcloth, a fabric like burlap, and sitting in ashes wasn't just an external expression. It was a way that people also turned their hearts to God. "Then I turned my face to the Lord God, seeking him by prayer and pleas for mercy with fasting and sackcloth and ashes" (ESV).

What personal events or situations in our world make you want to tear your clothes?

It's so bizarre that it's almost laughable that the king and Haman ordered a holocaust and then sat down for a cocktail. When Linda died, it would have been weird and inappropriate for me to be stoic, hiding my tears and sadness. It would have been horrifying for Mordecai and the Jews to face their annihilation with a plastic smile. And yet today, we're often unmoved by the pain around us.

Engaging our hearts in *good* grief is a start to bringing God's good into our world.

Pathway Principle

Grief is God's tool to join our hearts with His over what's broken.

Memorize

"Therefore, as God's chosen people, holy and dearly loved, clothe yourselves with compassion, kindness, humility, gentleness and patience" (Colossians 3:12).

Read the memory verse aloud four times. Read it very slowly the first time and faster each subsequent time.

Application

Evaluate your ability to grieve. What barriers to healthy grief have you experienced? Pray and ask God to open your heart to your own suffering and the suffering of others. Ask Him to remove the barriers.

Day Two: Feel All the Feels

As I turned off the news, I heaved a deep sigh. In thirty minutes, chaos and disaster unfolded before my eyes—pandemic, starvation, and natural disasters flooded my senses. I wanted to care about each, and every person represented in all the stories, but I just couldn't. After all, what could I, just one person, do? It was too overwhelming.

So, I turned to the pantry. An Oreo . . . or four . . . was surely the answer.

I'm exaggerating a little but not much. That opening story is based on something that happened in my house moments ago. It seems virtuous to contemplate the goodness of grief until it hits home. Then we just want it to Go Away.

Humans haven't changed much in all of history. Take a moment to reread Esther 4:2.

What caused Mordecai to have to stop at the king's gate?

Why do you think that was?

One way to study the Bible deeply is to read a passage over and over. On the fourth read of this passage, a dawning realization stopped me in my tracks. The king wouldn't let anyone dressed in sackcloth, those who were grieving, near him. Susa was where the royal court wintered, and from our reading in chapter 1, we know that the king had turned Susa into Party-Ville. There might as well have been a sign at the gate: Party People, Welcome! No Mourners Allowed.

Commentator Matthew Henry confirmed my insight in his writing, "Nothing but what was gay and pleasant must appear at court, and everything that was melancholy must be banished thence; all in king's palaces *wear soft clothing* (Matthew 11:8 ESV), not sackcloth."[2]

The king wasn't willing to hear the complaints of those in pain or grief. He only wanted what was happy and comfortable. How awful . . . and how like me with my Oreos.

Our current culture is all about comfort. We like things nice and neat. Cushy and comfy. Happy and peaceful. But when it's not, we're experts in what to do next. We turn to the nasty habit of numbing, because it feels so good to be shielded from what hurts so bad. There's a price to pay for numbing, though, and once we've seen it, we're less willing to pay it.

What We Trade for Comfort

Read Matthew 19:16–30. How is the young man described, and what does he want?

Why did the young man walk away sad?

What did he lose because of what he couldn't give up?

Based on what Jesus told Peter, what are we asked to give up? What comfort have those things brought to you?

But what does Jesus tell Peter that we get in return if we'll give up those things?

In the Bible, there are many people who give up deep connection with God and the joy that His purposes bring. They turn away because of the things that they can't give up, their own personal numbing agents.

Bible Nerd Box

Esau gives up God's blessing of birthright for some stew (Genesis 25). Balaam gives up hearing the word of the Lord for influence (Numbers 22–24). The tribes of Rueben and Gad give up the Promised Land for prime property on the other side of the Jordan (Numbers 32). John Mark gives up on the mission trip of a lifetime to return to the warm fires of home (Acts 15:36–38). I encourage you to dig into these riveting stories if you have time.

We'll look at Esther's response to the edict in coming days, but let's pause here a moment and consider what Esther's temptations might have been as she faced such harrowing news. It would have been natural for her to want to escape into the luxuries that a palace would offer—food, a plush bed to sleep her days away in, or the lull of entertainment. In her protected environment, it would have been easy for her to numb or escape. She could have sent the messengers away like the king and closed her windows to the wailing outside.

But she didn't. In sharp contrast to the king, Esther engaged with people's pain instead of hiding from it. Truly extraordinary.

Let's look at John 11:17–35 again. At first, who went to Jesus and who stayed at home?

In verse 31, what is the "ly" word that describes how Mary went when Jesus called to her?

Martha went directly to Jesus. Mary resisted at first, but she quickly went to Him when He called her by name. These sisters set a wonderful example for us when we're in pain.

When I was in my early thirties, I was the women's ministry director at my church, but I was inexperienced. A pastor wisely pointed me to a mentor, our church's secretary, Mona. When I went to Mona for advice, I could count on two things. She would direct me with Scripture instead of her own opinion, and she would always point me to Jesus. "Beloved, run to Jesus," was one of her oft-shared phrases, and it still echoes through my heart in times of crisis and grief.

In our humanity, we always have a choice.

Will we run to Jesus, or will we resist Him, turning to numbing instead?

When we resist Him, we often turn to *someone* to help us *deal* with things. As a friend said to me one time, "We run to the phone instead of the throne." These days, the phone is only one of dozens of ways that we can connect with other people instead of connecting with the One who can truly comfort us.

Who is someone you turn to that helps you deal with things?

We can also resist Him by running to *something* to *dull* our feelings. There are drugs, alcohol, and sex, but there are also substances that are more socially acceptable. The ones that "nice Christian girls" use—food (my confessed drug of choice) and an endless feed to scroll on our phones. Retail therapy, the temporary high of a purchase, is another dulling drug that made me flinch when I thought of it.

What is something that you've used to dull your feelings?

In and of themselves, the relationships that support us and the substances that comfort us aren't evil. It's when we misuse them to replace God Himself that the situation becomes problematic. The Bible has another name for the nasty numbing agents that we abuse to protect us from our own pain and the suffering of others. When we put our hope in objects or people instead of in God, they are called *idols.* Habakkuk 2:18–19 says it clearly, "Of what value is an idol carved by a craftsman? Or an image that teaches lies? For the one who makes it trusts in his own creation; he makes idols that cannot speak. Woe to him who says to wood, 'Come to life!' Or to lifeless stone, 'Wake up!' Can it give guidance? It is covered with gold and silver; there is no breath in it."

If this Scripture seems to have a muddy connection to the idea of numbing, I'll replace a few words with some of my numbing agents of choice. Then I challenge you to do the same.

"Of what value is an idol *baked* by a craftsman? Or an image that teaches lies? For the one who makes it trusts in his *sugary treat*; he makes idols that cannot speak. Woe to him who says to wood, *I have to have that beauty. Here's my credit card!'* Or to lifeless *phone*, 'Wake up!' Can it give guidance? It is *bedazzled* with gold and silver; there is no breath in it."

Scary, right? It pains me to do that exercise because I've fallen to those vain idols over and over again. Because I'm your friend, I hope it pierces your heart, too. Sorrow over our idols leads us to the best kind of grief. "For godly grief produces a repentance that leads to salvation without regret, whereas worldly grief produces death" (2 Corinthians 7:10 ESV).

King Xerxes numbed himself to the evil of his terrible decree with pleasure and happiness. He denied people's suffering and only listened to those who tickled his ears. He used his power and privilege to protect himself from the pain of others.

What if Mordecai and Esther had done the same by running away, hiding, or just ignoring the reality around them? The resulting disaster would have been too high of a price to pay for a few moments of comfort. Perhaps from hearing the stories of her people, Esther knew that the reward of running *at* her problem would be greater than the cost of running *from* it. She trusted the promises of God, spoken generations before, "Be strong and courageous. Do not be afraid or terrified because of them, for the Lord your God goes with you; he will never leave you nor forsake you" (Deuteronomy 31:6).

This is where we can use Esther as our shining example. She fully embraced faith instead of falling into her royal privilege. Following her, we turn toward the pain.

After all, friends, Esther had God's promises, but because of Jesus, we have *power*. He gifted us, those who believe, the overflowing fruits of the Spirit—"Love, joy, peace, forbearance, kindness, goodness, faithfulness, gentleness and self-control" (Galatians 5:22–23). He gave us the resurrection power and strength that resides within us (Ephesians 1:19–20).

How did she face the fearful edict without those supernatural tools? Scripture is vague, but there are some big clues in coming days, so make sure to watch for them.

We may not be dealing with the kind of tragedy that Mordecai and Esther were facing, but numbing is just as treacherous for our souls and the world around us. Not only is it the sin of idolatry, but God created human emotion so that our hearts would connect to His. Our emotions are to be a catalyst for righteous action. When we numb, we walk away from connection with God just like the rich young man, and we miss the Esther moments to serve others that God has created for us. Missing out on those two treasures would be tragic indeed.

Let's choose repentance instead, telling God we're sorry for numbing. Let's run to Jesus to wash off the idol dust that medicates us. Let's tear down our "no mourners allowed" signs, giving up our own power and privilege to leap into action for those who are suffering. Employing the spiritual strength and power that Jesus has given us, let's embrace the pain that's within us and around us so that we can step fully into the riches of deep relationship with God. The hurt God gives us to bear is hard sometimes, but it's so, so worth it.

Pathway Principle

Numbing is Satan's nasty strategy for keeping our hearts far from God.

Memorize

"Therefore, as God's chosen people, holy and dearly loved, clothe yourselves with compassion, kindness, humility, gentleness and patience" (Colossians 3:12).

Today, write out the memory verse four times and then read all four times aloud. Circle words that are meaningful to you.

Application

Pray and ask the Lord to show you how you've numbed instead of connected. Agree with what He shows you, confess, repent, and ask God to strip you of those idols.

How have you used power and privilege to protect yourself from others' pain?

Day Three: Feel the Fear and Lean In

As a recovering perfectionist, I struggle to process negative emotions, ones that I "shouldn't" be feeling. Historically, I haven't dealt well with anger, fear, bitterness, or hurt even though they're common human feelings. My lack of coping tools and resistance to negative emotions has often come back to bite me.

As a communicator, I especially love to speak and feel the connection with an audience. Some of my happiest moments are when I'm passing on transforming biblical truths to others. It's my sweet spot, because it's my calling. Not many people love to speak publicly, though, since there are the inevitable nerves from being in front. Over time and with experience, I've learned to manage the fear of public speaking, so generally, I don't let nerves overtake me before events anymore. A few years ago, I experienced a terrible exception.

Layered like a mountain on top of my calling to speak was a mound of negative emotions. Difficult circumstances and relational interactions built up one upon the other during the weeks before this particular event. The organizer had placed unfair expectations on my ability to draw a crowd at his church, and every conversation was laden with his disappointment in me. I was also sharing the stage with another speaker that I consider a rock star, and my insecurities started chipping away at my confidence. In addition to that, the night before the conference, I had an interaction with someone who berated and embarrassed me in a group.

The weight of all of it had taken a toll on me, but I didn't process any of it . . . until I was walking onto the stage to speak. At that unfortunate moment, all the feelings that I should have dealt with as each event happened—anger, insecurity, shame, resentment—came flooding over me in the form of overwhelming fear. When it came time to speak up, I was emotionally crashing down instead. Thirty minutes later, after a disastrous delivery, I wanted to disappear into a hole.

Have you ever been in a circumstance where unprocessed feelings all came crashing down at once? Summarize in a few sentences here.

Read Esther 4:4–11. What emotions are named in this passage?

Keeping Esther's humanness in mind, what must Esther have been feeling that isn't named? Think about the emotions that might have been attached to these circumstances and list them in the chart. A thesaurus may be useful to find words that express the layers of meaning.

Action	Emotion
Separation from Mordecai:	______________
Hearing about Mordecai in sackcloth:	______________
Not being able to talk to Mordecai directly:	______________
Not having unlimited access to her husband:	______________
Not being called to her husband in 30 days:	______________
Knowing her husband had access to 350 other women *and* he had disposed of his former wife: (Don't forget this doozy!)	______________

Crisis always brings about extremes in emotions, and Esther was in the direst circumstances. Regardless of action or inaction, her life was in danger, and her people had a contract out on them. If we were in her shoes, we can imagine that we wouldn't just be timid, we'd be terrified! Her feelings must have intensified as her understanding increased.

At first, her concern centered on Mordecai. The report about him from her maids threw her into "great distress," so she tried to care for his outward needs by sending him clothing. When he rejected her offering, she dug a little deeper, inquiring through Hathach about his inner being. She "ordered him to find out what was troubling Mordecai and why" (Esther 4:5).

Can you imagine how she felt when Hathach returned with Mordecai's reply? Her fear, focused on him initially, must have expanded inward when she heard both the details of the edict and Mordecai's *command* for her to go to the king. Some translations say that Mordecai "urged" her, but the truer translation is "commanded." It's easy to imagine that a growing panic, layered over fear, arose when she understood her position between a rock and a hard place.

Depict the deepening of Esther's emotions in this passage using words or a drawing.

When Fear Pushes Us in the Wrong Direction

Fear as a human emotion is first mentioned in Scripture near the origin of humankind. Although it wasn't present in the first days, when we were new creations walking sinlessly with God, it was the second emotion described after the first sin.

Read Genesis 3:1–12. What is the first negative human emotion expressed, but not named, in verse 7 immediately after Adam and Eve ate the fruit?

How did Adam and Eve feel at God's approach in verse 10?

What did Adam and Eve do because of this emotion?

While our natural, human reaction to fear is to run or hide, I have to give Esther props. Instead of hiding, Esther leaned in and continued the conversation with Mordecai.

Reread Esther 4:10–11. What were the details of the message that Esther sent back to Mordecai?

What's the worst possible outcome for Esther if she follows Mordecai's command to go before the king?

As I read and reread this passage in my study Bible, a word inserted by a commentator in the right margin caught my eye—selfishness. Really?! Esther was being selfish in recounting the facts to Mordecai? Historians and theologians alike corroborate Persian kings were protected as human deities by restricting access to them. After all, as we studied yesterday, some unwanted folks might bring news that would pop the king's lovely bubble. Herodotus himself wrote of this law.

Bible Nerd Box

Only seven men in the court known as the king's "friends" were permitted to "see the face of the king." Herodotus explains that only they could enter the king's presence unannounced, except when he was sleeping with a woman.[3] Haman was one of these seven men. He had access to the king when Esther did not.

As a lay-theologian, I respectfully disagree. Esther wasn't selfish in her reply. She was wise. When we're given a calling, there are costs and sacrifices that go hand-in-hand with the commitment. As Lynn says, "Caring costs something." Just as Esther faced the potential loss of her life, the ultimate penalty, entering into others' suffering will cost us, too. The cost of caring can include time, finances, and even our reputation. We probably won't be called into Esther's shoes where caring could cost our lives, but it's not out of the realm of possibility.

Esther surely felt fear, but she didn't try to hide, run, or avoid. She leaned in and pragmatically counted the costs. If she was selfish, she would have refused, but verse 11 seems to have the dual purpose of reminding Mordecai of the potential consequences and processing them herself.

Think of a time in the past that you acted because of caring. Name the reason that you cared and what you did in response. (i.e., Your parent that you love had an illness, and you took time off work to care for them during recovery.)

____

____

____

____

What were the costs of your caring action? Consider all the angles—financial, emotional, time, etc.

____

____

____

____

Esther faced her fear, not defaulting to numbing or allowing it to derail her. She used it instead to give her clear-eyed focus. Despite her fear, she heard the cries of her people, trusted their faithful God, and faced the direst of outcomes without flinching. How can we do the same?

All the Feels and How to Face Them

When my oldest son, Anson, was a freshman in high school, he went to our church's fall retreat. This annual event held at a nearby camp was one our whole youth group anticipated. Twelve months of the year, the kids raved about the food fight, the fun water sports, and the zipline speed. Before I knew it, Anson was boarding the bus along with the rest of the gang, smiling from ear to ear.

That Sunday morning, I got a call with news that sent chills through me. One of the seniors, a popular boy renowned for fun and a deep love for Jesus, had fallen from the zipline and died from his injuries. His life ebbed away even as horrified camp counselors, youth leaders, and kids looked on. It was a horrendous loss that rocked our church to its core.

In an effort to help everyone process their grief, our church leadership brought in a professional Christian counselor to speak to a group of our youth leaders, kids, and parents. I will never forget one thing that the counselor told us. He explained that Christians are amongst his hardest patients to treat because of how we deny our feelings, believing wrongly that faith should protect us from negative emotions. The advice that followed is some I've been trying to live into ever since. "Feel all your feelings," he told us, "and then lay them at the foot of the cross."

Anger is not wrong. Fear is not bad. It's what we do with those emotions that can become a liability. Thankfully, Jesus is the Savior who understands every emotion that we experience. We're blessed with a gift that Esther couldn't have even imagined!

Read Hebrews 2:17–18 and 4:14–15. What does it mean that Jesus was "fully human in every way"?

How does knowing that Jesus walked through everything you've walked through and more help you process your circumstances and feelings today?

Feeling is not selfishness. It's not weakness or a lack of faith. We need not fear our feelings. We can experience them all without wallowing by bringing them to Jesus, our Savior who understands. He felt anger at injustice (John 2:13–16). He's felt the pain of betrayal (Luke 22:47–48). He's felt the fear of death (Matthew 26:42).

What feelings have you been stuffing down that you need to bring to Jesus?

What feelings have you been wallowing in that you need to bring to Jesus?

Because we have the advantage of foresight, we can cheer wildly for Esther in this moment. She felt the legitimate fear of losing her life, counted the cost, and made the right decision. Esther shows us the way to step into fearful things. She feared, but she obeyed anyway.

We don't have to hide or stuff our negative emotions like I did before my speaking event. Not only is it unhealthy to behave that way, it's downright destructive.

Instead of stuffing, we can surrender our emotions to the One who understands them and empowers us to face them.

He alone is the one who strengthens us to transition from caring to acting.

Pathway Principle

When we surrender our fears to God, we can obey anyway.

Memorize

Today, fill in the blanks. Then read the verse aloud into a recording device. Listen to it four times while you're reading it.

"Therefore, as God's__________ people, __________and dearly loved, clothe yourselves with ____________, kindness, _____________, gentleness and __________" (Colossians 3:12).

Application

What fears have you been stuffing instead of surrendering?

____

____

____

____

____

Have any of these fears kept you from caring for others well? If so, tell how.

Take a moment to acknowledge, feel them, and then write out a prayer, surrendering each one to Jesus. Lay them at the foot of the cross.

Day Four: Feel the Joy of Joining God

Questions from the conference wouldn't go away. I had listened to the stream of a panel discussion as I walked, and my mind was swirling. "Who's going to be here in thirty days? Who will be here in sixty days?" Reggie, the panel coordinator had asked.

The panel discussion was on the topic of race in America, and it was held after a horrific and unjust string of African Americans' deaths. In the aftermath, hearts were open and even eager to learn, but Reggie was justifiably skeptical after years in the work of racial equity. She knew that lots of people were ready to join the movement at the moment, but as time went by the hoard would dwindle, distracted by other news of the day. But I couldn't stop thinking about her question. Would I still be committed to learning, growing, and seeking solutions in thirty days? In sixty?

In the silence, I heard the Spirit whisper, "Amy, help women be there in thirty days." My mind raced as a vision grew, but surely God couldn't mean *me.*

I'm not ready, Lord! I'm new at this, and I don't know enough, I argued.

But the thoughts that I knew weren't my own continued, "I've been preparing you for almost three years, Amy."

A peace washed over me. God was right as usual! I had been taking classes about racial equity, attending conferences, joining a diverse supper club created to build understanding, and nurturing friendships with wise women of color—gifts straight from God. I was no expert, but I was ahead of many who wanted to learn. I knew it was going to be difficult, but with the help of some experienced friends, I started a month-long private Facebook group called "30 Days Toward Unity and Love."

Describe a time that you've been called to do something that was clearly beyond you.

Read Esther 4:12–14. Modecai's words in this passage have been hotly debated amongst commentators. How do you interpret his meaning?

Many commentators see his message as an ominous threat toward Esther. They believe that he's warning her that he'll "out" her as a Jew if she doesn't obey his command to go to the king.

I don't believe this is the case. Although Esther had hidden her Jewish identity from many, surely her maids and even the eunuchs must have been clued in because of her close communication with Mordecai. He had revealed his own Jewish identity at the gate, and Esther had shown her love for him. This saying reinforces my viewpoint, "Two people can keep a secret if one of them is dead." If the household staff knew that Esther was a Jew, or had guessed that was the case, it wouldn't be a secret for long when it was time for the Jews to be killed.

"In Mordecai's thinking, Esther's life *may* be in jeopardy if she goes to the king uninvited, but her doom is *certain* if she does not."[4] This assessment is true no matter how you interpret Mordecai's words.

Mordecai, Mugs, and T-Shirts

Verse 14 ends with the words most quoted from the book of Esther. "And who knows but that you have come to your royal position for such a time as this?"

Mordecai's words are favorites for mugs and t-shirts. They make us feel inspired and special. How our straying hearts want a tiara. Oh, how we *long* for a tiara! In our Disney-driven world, we tend to respond *I'm a princess, too!* when we read these words, but that's a gross misinterpretation.

Instead of pointing at the Queen's attributes, this may be the clearest gesture toward our hidden God in this book. Mordecai isn't telling Esther that she's the one. That she's special. He's not telling her, "Now's the time to unleash your hidden potential!"

Instead, he's pointing her back to our Sovereign God. The Creator who spoke the worlds into existence is the same One who has created a queen from a humble Jewess. He alone positioned her in the palace where she could save her people. Neither she nor Mordecai could have foreseen this purpose, but God did. The same God who created Esther, with her unique set of gifts, put her in this place and circumstance with a call to fulfill His redeeming plan. God gave Esther a unique usefulness, and He gives you one, too.

Our unique usefulness is expressed beautifully in Ephesians 2:10, "For we are God's handiwork, created in Christ Jesus to do good works, which God prepared in advance for us to do." Your unique usefulness is, like Esther, the good works God had in mind when He created you, and it's not necessarily what you've pursued or desired.

In reference to her influence in an interview, Karen Swallow Prior, English professor and influencer, said, "It is what God called me to because *that call came from outside* . . . It was not ever what I imagined or asked for or wanted."[5] (my emphasis added)

Esther's place of usefulness in God's Kingdom wouldn't have been what she would have asked for since it involved risking her life. Karen Swallow Prior didn't ask for influence that involved the hate of social media trolls or the questioning of her integrity. Occasionally, though, our unique usefulness is a huge leap of faith like Esther's or Karen's.

However, our call from the outside, our unique usefulness, isn't usually what we'd dreamed of either. Our "for such a time as this" isn't the "big thing" but rather the small, everyday task. It's taking a meal to a sick neighbor who needs to feel God's love. It's the behind-the-scenes volunteer position in our community. It's advocating for the voiceless over coffee instead of a position of notoriety.

Let me say the last paragraph back to you, and you fill your name in the blank.

> ___________, who knows whether you have not come to the kingdom for such a time as this? Our sovereign God, the Creator who spoke the worlds into existence is the same one who created you, positioning you in a place where you can save people—their souls and maybe even their bodies. You couldn't have foreseen this purpose, but God did. The same God who created you, ________, with your unique set of gifts, put you in this place and circumstance with a call to fulfill His redeeming plan. You have a unique usefulness.

What is your gut-level response to knowing that you have a unique usefulness?

Esther's purpose was pointed out to her by Mordecai. Do you have anyone pointing out your purpose to you? Who? What are they saying?

God used Esther's life, and He wants to use yours, too.

The Amazing Thing About Miracles

Although God is a God of miracles, it's interesting that miracles are another missing element in the book of Esther. God certainly could have dealt with King Xerxes and Haman all by Himself if He had chosen to do so.

Read Daniel 5, an account of how God interacted with one of King Xerxes predecessors. What miraculous way does God appear in this story?

What is the result of God's judgement on King Belshazzar?

Although Daniel is *part* of this story, he isn't the *agent of action* in this particular narrative. God does the work all by Himself, and He could have done it that way in the book of Esther, too. Again and again, God did incredible miracles to save His people like judging through plagues (Exodus 6–13), parting the Red Sea (Exodus 14), providing food from heaven (Exodus 16), or bringing water from the rock (Exodus 17).

In Esther, God accomplished His redeeming work in a different way. His Providence was fulfilled through an ordinary woman. God certainly moved to place Esther where she was, but His work of saving His people in this circumstance was done through her, not around her. It was a quieter work, and it depended on her obedience. While Esther had maintained a split identity for years, secret Jew and public Queen, she now had to merge the two to step into God's story. Being both obedient and true to whom she was became the secret sauce to fulfilling her unique usefulness.

How has obedience played a role in fulfilling God's plans for you?

How has He used your truest, God-created self to accomplish it—your talents, gifts, and personality?

If Esther hadn't accomplished her purpose, the consequences would have been dire. Although Mordecai said that "relief and deliverance will rise for the Jews from another place," the threat of annihilation was real.

Maybe the greater danger was the loss of intimacy with God through disobedience, a hardening of the heart and the devastating emotions of a lost opportunity.

Esther was at the moment of decision. She had to choose. Would she earn the joy that comes through obedience, even when it's risky, or would she carry the weight of regret and shame?

As always, Jesus is our ultimate example of the human experience. Counterintuitively, He experienced His greatest gain in His most terrible moment. Hebrews 12:2 tells us, ". . . looking to Jesus, the founder and perfecter of our faith, who for the joy that was set before him endured the cross, despising the shame, and is seated at the right hand of the throne of God" (ESV). Through His obedience on the cross, Jesus experienced the joy of looking forward to our salvation. Esther had the choice to embrace the joy offered to her through risky obedience or to walk away from it.

Describe a time that you faced risky obedience. Did you obey or walk away? What was the resulting feeling?

____

____

____

____

As I've studied the book of Esther, my excitement has grown. She's so much like us, an ordinary woman designed with a unique usefulness, walking in the Providence of God without a miracle in sight.

Esther's obedience joined with God's providence *was* the miracle.

It's the same for us. We're not to sit passively by, waiting for God to bring it all to pass without us. We're to wait and watch, stepping into the risky obedience of our unique usefulness when God makes it evident. In that moment, we become the miracle.

Pathway Principle

You were created with a unique usefulness that's your part in God's story.

Memorize

Today, fill in the blanks. Once you're finished, read it aloud once while clapping your hands in rhythm.

"Therefore, as God's____________ people, ____________and dearly loved, clothe yourselves with ______________, kindness, ________________, gentleness and ____________" (Colossians 3:12).

Now try to say it aloud without looking. Don't worry about mistakes. Just use it as an opportunity to see what your brain hasn't "caught" yet. Read the sections aloud that you had trouble with several more times.

Application

Consider your past, present, and future when you're working to identify your unique usefulness. Let's use Esther as an example first.

Past—Esther's foundational identity was as a Jew, one of God's chosen people. Because of her upbringing, she had a loyalty and empathy for her people.

Present—Her present position as Queen had both prepared and positioned her to make a difference.

Future—We may not face anything as extreme as Esther faced, but her future, her very life, depended upon knowing and stepping into her unique usefulness.

Our unique usefulness changes over the course of our lives. It's not just one and done. Esther's unique usefulness in her season of crisis was to act on behalf of her people, but later it may have been becoming an example of godliness for her children or caring for an aging Mordecai.

Now consider your own unique usefulness for this season of your life.

Past: Write down gifts, talents, experiences, etc., that have prepared you for what God has for you to do today.

Present: Write down a present need, crisis, or suffering that God is bringing to your attention. It is probably right where you are or something that has been tugging at your heart over and over. What do you have that you can offer—time, expertise, finances, training?

Future: Write down your dreams for how your future and others' will look if you step into your unique usefulness.

Don't be discouraged if you left some of this blank or if you still don't know what your unique usefulness is. Keep the question open between you and God, and ask Him to show you how He wants to use you and your one beautiful life. He is delighted by your open heart, and He wants you to feel the joy of walking in your unique usefulness!

Day Five: Feel the Urgency to Act

Sometimes there's a catalyst for action, a turning point that you just can't ignore. One of the training grounds for the "30 Days Toward Unity & Love" was the MLK50 Conference that I attended. It was a conference hosted by the Gospel Coalition memorializing Martin Luther King Jr.'s assassination by talking about race in the church. God used that conference to clarify His calling on me in a way that was *almost* irresistible.

But I was scared. Because . . .

The problem is so big.
I'm just one person.
I don't know enough to get involved.

Although my feelings of hesitancy were real, they must have paled in comparison to what Esther felt in her turning-point moment. Even when we long to allow God to use our unique usefulness to be part of God's story, there's always a list of potential pitfalls that can hold us back.

Ask God to help you see the truth about yourself, to be completely honest, and then circle the reasons that you've chosen numbing over acting. There are different reasons in different circumstances, so think about several turning-points that you have faced.

Too overwhelmed with my own circumstances	Too many unknowns
Enough to do in my own world	Upsets my status quo
The problem's not like my experiences, so "not real"	Would make me an outsider in my own group
Threatens my own happiness	Insecure in my ability to help
Afraid of how much it will take	Desire to maintain my own comfort
Makes me uncomfortable	Has potential consequences that I don't want

Read Esther 4:15–17. What is Esther's final decision? What does she say that lets you know it's final?

What directions does she give to Mordecai?

Esther may have been a reluctant advocate, but in a moment of need and crisis, she came through. She would go to the king and speak up for her life and the life of her people, the Jews.

advocate (noun)
**ad - vo - cate | \ ˈad-və-kət , -ˌkāt **

1. one who pleads the cause of another
2. one who defends or maintains a cause or proposal
3. one who supports or promotes the interests of a cause or group[6]

Do you see yourself in the definition above? Have you ever felt your unique usefulness was to advocate for a person, a cause, or a group? Describe the situation.

What obstacles did you have to overcome to become an advocate?

What feelings did you have when you stepped into that role?

Tool #1: Asking for the Wonders of Wisdom

It's amazing to watch Esther step into her purpose as an advocate with such wisdom. Her clarity, command, and decisive action is jarring after all the hesitancy. Esther felt her need for support, though, and she asked for it. There can only be one source for that kind of transformation—the One who was calling her. Esther's ability to move forward in wisdom points directly to God.

What do these verses tell us about wisdom? Draw a line from the verse to the truth.

James 1:5	God gives wisdom to the upright and protection to those with integrity.
Psalm 111:10	God gives wisdom generously when we ask.
Proverbs 2:7	Fear of the Lord is where wisdom begins.

Proverbs 2:7 hints at something interesting. "He stores up sound wisdom for the upright; he is a shield to those who walk in integrity" (ESV). I wonder. *Had Esther grown in her relationship with God, becoming a more upright woman of integrity, while she lived in the palace?* Based on the evidence here, I believe it's possible. She certainly employed four Kingdom tools, strategies that all of God's people can use, that we find throughout Scripture. The first is that she had clearly asked for wisdom.

Tool #2: Mobilizing the Courage of Community

When God calls us into hard things, He almost always provides community for resources and support. He provided Aaron and Hur to hold up Moses' arms during a battle (Exodus 17:12). He gave Jonathon's friendship to sustain David during his wait for the crown (1 Samuel 18:1). God sent Mary to Elizabeth after the angel's message that she was carrying the Messiah (Luke 1:39–45). He arranged for Paul to meet Lydia who was the host for his Philippian church plant (Acts 16:11–16).

The list could go on and on, but Scripture's message is clear. We weren't created to do life or hard things alone. God has given us the gift of community, and power resides there. In my own life, I've watched in awe as my people-magnet friend, Cary, has grown her non-profit that empowers and advocates for women coming out of vulnerable circumstances. She hasn't tried to do it alone. Instead, Designed for Joy is flourishing because of the way Cary reaches out to others when she has a gap or need. Her partners not only encourage her, they also bring their unique gifts, services, and resources.

In the same way, Esther wisely mobilized her community, serving them and certainly drawing strength from them. It grew with each step in this chapter, and she did it in response to what she was feeling. She felt distressed about Mordecai, so she looped in Hathach the eunuch. Her continued concern about Mordecai's grief causes her to pursue him, the one who had always been on her team. In the final harrowing moment of decision, Esther employed her maids and got Mordecai to bridge her to the whole Jewish community, vanquishing her fear with communal strength. Esther was a woman who recognized the power of the community around her and reached out with confidence to gather them.

Who is currently part of your community who encourages you—strengthens your unique usefulness and advocacy?

____

____

____

____

Who helps you to overcome the fear of moving forward?

____

____

____

____

____

Pause a moment to pray. Who is God calling you to pursue to be part of your community?

____

____

____

Tool #3: Harnessing the Fortitude of Fasting

In the pattern that Lynn and I see in Esther, we've covered "listen" and "feel," but there's one step on the pathway that Esther shows us that we shouldn't bypass. Before we leap into doing, we fast.

For many of us, fasting is an unfamiliar practice. On a trip to India almost twenty years ago, my team and I were prayer-walking through the red-light district of Calcutta where the ravages of poverty and prostitution are overwhelming. A pastor who was leading his church to reach out to the women living in these horrifying conditions explained to us how his church laid the foundation for this ministry. They had prayed and fasted for two years before beginning the "do" of outreach into this dangerous region. Two years?! In my American way of thinking, two minutes of fasting seems like a lot.

I'm realizing that my well-fed ways leave a spiritual starvation. It's an emptiness that can only be filled with turning to God in the way He prescribes.

Fasting fills us, unleashing the Holy Spirit who sustains us.

Even when we're called by God, our own enthusiasm for doing will run out. We must be empowered by the Holy Spirit.

When Jesus' disciples ran into a situation that was too hard for them, when nothing they did worked for casting a demon out of a young boy, Jesus clearly outlined the solution. "So He said to them, 'This kind can come out by nothing but prayer and fasting'" (Mark 9:29 NKJV).

Have you ever fasted? If so, write about your experience here.

Just like the church in Calcutta, Esther paused in the midst of an urgent situation to fast. Surely this is a hint that Esther's reliance on God is growing! She also called others to join her, a plea for a power-boost. In his book, *The Fasting Edge*, pastor Jentezen Franklin says we often want God to use us. We ask Him to show us how and where; we're ready to go. In our excitement [and might I add impatience], we don't do the work to prepare to be used by God. We just want to get started. Once we get started, our lack of preparation slows us down. Pastor Franklin says we need to see: "Fasting is slowing down to speed up. It's taking time to listen for your next set of instructions from the throne."[7]

Zechariah 4:6b says, "Not by might, nor by power, but by my Spirit, says the Lord of hosts" (ESV). Fasting is one powerful way to bring God's Spirit into our doing. Esther recognized that her next steps were perilous and too big for her to accomplish on her own.

She fought her fear with fasting and won the prize of obedience.

In Isaiah 58:6–11, what does God say is the purpose for fasting? What are the results when we fast God's way?

What circumstance in your life might you need to fast for today?

Tool #4: Digging Into the Power of Pre-Deciding

Esther's last recorded words before diving into doing are a battle-cry for the undecided. "If I perish, I perish." Do you hear the echo of some others in God's story who had decided to follow God no matter the consequences?

Read Daniel 3:16–18. Why were these three men being threatened, and what were they facing?

Combined with Esther's bold statement, "If I perish, I perish," what emotions and decisions does their response stir in you?

We have the advantage of hindsight. It's easy for those of us who know the end of the story to simply say, "Oh, Esther will be fine. It's a happy ending with a holiday attached!" But Esther didn't have our point of view. The pink bow on top of her story wasn't secured yet. Even so, she mastered her fears and pre-decided that doing what was right was a reward in and of itself. Following in God's footsteps would take her to the best destination, even if it meant her death.

There are times in our walk with God that demand a decision. In fact, a pre-decision is a priceless tool in times of crisis. It's that moment for us right now in this study. Will we follow God no matter what? No matter where He takes us or what He asks of us? No matter who is threatening or the terrible things that might come?

The action stirred in my heart at the MLK50 conference led me to some of the hardest interactions of my life. But can I share with you? God's hardest places are still the best. They're infused with the joy and peace of His Presence, so there's no place better. Esther knew in her heart that the Psalmist's words are true, "Better is one day in your courts than a thousand elsewhere; I would rather be a doorkeeper in the house of my God than dwell in the tents of the wicked" (Psalm 84:10). Esther's choice could have led her out of the palace into a tomb, but she knew that God would meet her there. Her pre-decision strengthened her.

Seeking wisdom, building community, fasting, and pre-deciding are the Kingdom tools that He's handed us to manage our emotions before we dive into our unique usefulness. As we head into next week, let's take them up and wield them with confidence as we step into doing.

Pathway Principle

God clears the way to our unique usefulness with His empowering kingdom tools.

Memorize

"Therefore, as God's chosen people, holy and dearly loved, clothe yourselves with compassion, kindness, humility, gentleness and patience" (Colossians 3:12).

Today, cover our memory verse with your hand and repeat it four times. Peek without shame if you need to!

Application

Which of the Kingdom tools do you need to strengthen you today as you prayerfully step toward the doing of your unique usefulness?

Feel Pathway Principles

God uses human emotion to connect our hearts to His as a catalyst for righteousness and action.

- Grief is God's tool to join our hearts with His over what's broken.
- Numbing is Satan's nasty strategy for keeping our hearts far from God.
- When we surrender our fears to God, we can obey anyway.
- You were created with a unique usefulness that's your part in God's story.
- God clears the way to our unique usefulness with His empowering kingdom tools.

Prayer

Lord, I believe that You have created me for such a time as this. You've given me a unique usefulness, and I want to leverage my emotions to step into the Kingdom work that You have for me. Calm my fears and help me to pre-decide to follow You no matter what may come. In Jesus' name, Amen.

Questions for Discussion or Personal Journaling

1. Describe a time that someone cared for you in a sacrificial way, in a way that cost them something. How did it make you feel?

2. How did the section about God's feelings impact you? Make you see Him differently?

3. God often uses pain in the world to spur us to action or point out a problem. How have you seen this in the news this month or in your personal life?

4. What is one new thing you learned directly from the Scripture reading this week?

5. Which of the ideas from this week resonated with you the most? How will you apply this idea in your life next week?

Do

Day One: But Do We Know How It Will Turn Out?

Hi there! It's Lynn again. Remember me? The speedster who's learning better listening skills?

As we head into chapters 5 and 6 of Esther this week, we will learn from Esther as she moves forward. First, we saw how she listened. Then how she felt. Now it's go-time—time for Esther to *do*. This doing will be directly linked to Esther's obedience.

Have you ever been in the crux between obeying God and a potentially scary outcome?

As a young professional, I found myself on my knees. My husband was struggling to find work, both that fit his desires and his training. Each morning, I would kneel in my clothes closet, taking Matthew 6:6 very literally. I was asking the Lord for a new job for Greg, praying specifically for the type he wanted.

One day while praying, I sensed a nudge: "The specifics you are praying for fit *your* job. Your job is Greg's job." *Did I hear that right? Really? My job is the job for Greg?*

I had recently obtained my first sales position, what I thought was my dream job. It involved every aspect of what I thought I would enjoy so when it was offered to me, I had happily said "yes." To prepare for this outside sales work, my new employer had asked me to spend a couple of weeks inside the office, learning each piece of the business. I was in this season of training when I had this thought while praying.

As odd as it felt and as scared as I was, I sensed God's hand might be behind this crazy idea.

Driving to work that day, I prepared to present this idea to my boss. As I did, all types of scenarios flitted through my mind. *What if my boss thinks I'm asking him to interview Greg because I don't think I have what it takes? What if he thinks I am asking because I don't want the job? What if he doesn't hire Greg but still decides he wants someone else to fill the role? What if my seeming uncertainty gives him reason to let me go?*

That day, when I went to work and asked my boss if he would consider interviewing my husband for my job, I wish you could have seen the confusion on his face! I proposed interviewing Greg for my outside sales position, and I could fill an empty administrative role. My boss made sure I knew what I stood to lose; I would have a pay cut and the outside sales position would no longer be available to me. I understood. He interviewed Greg and had him take a few tests. Soon Greg and I both had new jobs. Greg in the outside sales role and me as an administrative assistant, a job that I really enjoyed. As of today, Greg has been with this company for thirty-three years!

While Esther isn't trying to decide between obeying God and losing her dream job, she is at a point of monumental risk.

When we last left Esther, she had called for a fast for herself, her young women as well as all the Jews to be found in Susa (Esther 4:16). This scene is one of "high dramatic tension,"[1] the "make it or break it" risk of going before the king.

Sometimes when we read God's Word, we see these stories as so big we have a hard time bringing them down to our every day. While taking a risk of giving up your dream job is not the same as going before a king and possible death, it was a climax in my real-life story. I had spent time reading God's Word and learning how to listen to Him, but there comes a time when the listening and feeling have to move forward in maturity. I had to actually do what I had been learning about: obey.

Doing sounds like a great adventure when reading a story like Esther or clapping for a great point in a sermon, but the space in time that comes right after the enthusiasm is the place where we can slowly stall out. The listening and feeling never transition to doing the good works God has called us to (Ephesians 2:10).

Esther listened and felt. Now it's time to take the risk and in her own words, "if I perish, I perish." Esther, "who with reluctance has taken up a cause for the purpose of saving others" moves forward.[2]

Read Esther 5:1–8. While reading this passage, write out each action word. (I found 7.)

On the third day of the fast, Esther "put on her royal robe." While praying is not mentioned directly, it is typically associated with fasting. The spiritual preparation has been done. The time for waiting is up. Whether she feels courageous and confident or she's doing it scared, Esther makes her way to the king's inner court.

Esther made it clear to Mordecai that she didn't know how she would be received. In the past, assertive women didn't fare so well with King Xerxes. In a society that believed men to be superior to women, women were expected to follow a man . . . no matter what. Yet, Esther is willing to take the risk for the sake of the people God loves. While she may be trembling under those royal robes, I believe she is leaning into discernment and looking for God to make the king receptive toward her.

When have you experienced a time when you sensed God directing you to move, but you didn't feel confident of the outcome?

Describe the type of posture Esther took as described in Esther 5:1.

While Esther has heard of the royal procedure of the king holding out his golden scepter, it's safe to assume it's a protocol she's not experienced before. The consequences, should the king choose *not* to hold out the golden scepter, was death (Esther 4:11). Can you possibly imagine the relief engulfing Esther as the king began raising his arm? Not only was he not offended; he was glad to see her.

Oh, the kindness of God when the worst-case scenario doesn't play out as we have imagined. And even greater, when the thing we feared most of all never comes to pass and God surprises us with the good we desire instead.

Getting past things that scare me isn't my favorite thing to do, yet I have had a lifetime of learning to do just that. This motivation to overcome fear actually comes from another fear—the fear of God.

I began learning about the fear of God in my late teens in a Christian discipleship training program. In recent years I've learned from some women who get a lot less facetime in the Bible than Esther: Shiphrah and Puah in Exodus 1. These two women were also interacting with a king and the outcome of their actions would also determine the future of God's people.

The Pharaoh of Egypt, in a display of insecurity, commands these two midwives to kill Jewish boys before the babies take their first breath. Recognizing the responsibility they have to their people and to obey their God, "The midwives, however, feared God and did not do what the king of Egypt had told them to do; they let the boys live" (Exodus 1:17).

The word translated *fear* in verse 17 is quite different from the type of fear Esther may have experienced standing in the inner court of the king's palace. The fear Shiphrah and Puah had is the Hebrew word *yare* which can mean to be afraid, be frightened, to revere, to respect, or to be awesome. It is a fear that comes from a combination of love, hope, and reverence, not extreme apprehension.[8]

While you and I are probably not going before kings and pharaohs to save our nations, our fear of God—our love, hope, and reverence for Him—partnered with the Holy Spirit, needs to be the power behind our doing behind our works.

Why does James 2:14–26 tell us *doing* is our next move?

As James tells us, doing good works is an outflow of our faith in God. Esther's move to advocate for her people didn't *cause* her to be a child of God. She took her courageous step because she *was* a child of God.

Our works are not our identity. Our work is the *outflow* of our identity.

Good work is your identity put into action.

Like Esther's uncertainty in going before the king, we have no idea how our steps with God will turn out. While physical death is not what most of us face, we may risk the death of control of our schedules, our reputations, our futures, and certainly our comfort levels.

This is something we need to grapple with as we move forward.

As we've been progressing through the story of Esther, we're each progressing through our own stories of being used by God. For some of us, now, like Esther, it's time to move . . . to *do* what He calls us to do. For Esther, her first move produced an outcome she hoped for—the king delighted to see her.

But let's not hurry to get to the good parts, overlooking what is so important: Esther did what was right not knowing if it would turn out right. *Lord, help us to do the same! To obey You and do what You are calling us to do, whether it turns out the way we're hoping or not!*

Pathway Principle

We can choose what is right even in uncertainty, not knowing if it will turn out right.

Memorize

"Dear friends, let us love one another, for love comes from God. Everyone who loves has been born of God and knows God. Whoever does not love does not know God, because God is love" (1 John 4:7–8).

Read the memory verse aloud four times. Read it very slowly the first time and faster each subsequent time.

Application

What is one thing you can do to move toward something you sense God might be asking you to do?

____

____

____

____

Day Two: What Do You Want?

Have you ever had a time when obeying God was downright painful? Did it feel like it would be the undoing of you?

Part of my story reads like a teen romance novel, filled with angst and emotional curves. As a young girl, I met a boy at church. I didn't really know him, but he liked me and when you're eleven years old, that's about all that matters. Now this boy was not your usual boy with a usual crush. In fact, I later learned he wrote in his Bible, "I will marry Lynnette Martin, to be stopped by nobody." (That's me!)

As crushes go, this infatuation faded as he moved into middle school. But mine only grew. I think it had something to do with that "first love" thing. They say first love can impact us profoundly when our brains are young and still developing. Our thoughts and actions sometimes mimic an addiction. All through my teen years, this boy was my crush. In the meantime, he went on to college, dated someone for many years, and apparently moved on.

After high school, I went to a short-term discipleship training school, preparing students for a lifetime of serving Jesus. Who should contact me while I was one thousand miles from home? The boy-now-man, asking if he could come and visit. *Can you even try to imagine how ecstatic my still infatuated heart was?* And yet, I knew I had committed this season of my life to giving Jesus everything. I also knew if I told him not to come, this might be my only chance to have the relationship I desperately wanted.

I had a choice to make. Was I going to say yes to his visit or yes to only pursuing Jesus at this time? It came down to whom I was going to please. Myself? The young man? Or the One I said had my whole heart?

After spending time with Jesus, crying until I could cry no more, I made up my mind to obey God. I wrote the "do not come" letter, moving in obedience.

Read Esther 5.

In Esther 5, Esther came to the point of decision.

After approaching the king, she finds he is delighted to see her. Then the king asked, "What is it, Queen Esther? What is your request? Even up to half the kingdom, it will be given you" (Esther 5:3). While to you and I this appears to be overly generous, it is in fact, a usual response among kings, when their hearts are open to another person. They are giving the freedom to ask. As long as it's reasonable, the answer is yes![4]

Advancing wisely, Esther seeks to serve before asking for anything. ". . . If it pleases the king, let the king and Haman come today to a feast that I have prepared for the king" (Esther 5:4 ESV). Esther begins her big move with serving her community, the king, and even her enemy, Haman. She follows the godly principle Jesus would one day give to us all: ". . . Whoever wants to become great among you must be your servant" (Matthew 20:26).

Moving through Esther 5, the King, Haman and Esther are now enjoying their after-dinner drink when the king asks Esther again, "What is your wish?"

What *does* Esther want?

Ultimately, she wants her people saved. She wants what is true, just, and fair for them. Without intervention, God's people will be annihilated. As a representative for her people, she steps into the space of responsibility.

A major theme running through the book of Esther is human responsibility. Both Mordecai and Esther demonstrate they understand what God expects of them as His people (Esther 2:19–23). Esther demonstrates responsibility again as she gains an audience with the king (Esther 5:1–8).

Not only is responsibility a theme in the book of Esther, but responsibility is also one of the facets of biblical justice as described in God's Word. Pastor Tim Keller states that biblical justice is characterized by responsibility, generosity, equality, and advocacy.[5]

Part of doing good works is bringing God's biblical justice to our world. We become part of Jesus' prayer, "Your kingdom come, your will be done" (Matthew 6:10).

Let's look at each of these four facets briefly.

1. Responsibility

What is our responsibility as slaves of God? (Romans 1:1)

Read Jesus' words in Mark 12:30–31. What does He command us to do?

Before Esther went to the king, she asked her people to fast with her. In Isaiah 58:6–14, God describes the type of fast He desires of us.

Reread Isaiah 58:6–14, the passage Amy had you read last week. Ask the Holy Spirit to reveal what He wants you to see. List the specific actions, the doing, God describes in this passage.

List the results of this doing in Isaiah 58:6–14 and the promise God gives in verse 11.

Read Deuteronomy 10:17–19. List the people described. What do they all have in common?

____

____

____

____

List the words associated in conjunction with vulnerable people. What type of words are used to describe them?

____

____

____

____

The words used in Deuteronomy 10:17–19 are all actions: executes, gives, sets free, opens, lifts up, loves, watches, upholds. I want to be like God. I want to partner with God to execute, give, set free, open blind eyes, lift up, love, watch, and uphold.

Many of us are not impacted by the injustices listed in this passage. As a result, we simply choose to go about our lives, busy with the responsibilities we already are laden with—caregiving, church, and careers. On many days, these responsibilities can feel like more than we can handle.

I am challenged by the words of Reverend Sylvester "Tee" Turner, "For those of us not impacted by social, economic, religious, governmental, or financial prejudice, we have the luxury of ignoring what doesn't hurt us. But do we really? Not if we love and serve and follow God. Amos 5:24 tells us, 'But let justice roll down like waters, and righteousness like an ever-flowing stream'"[6] (ESV).

Esther, as Queen of Persia, could have gone about her comfortable life as long as her heritage was unknown. But upon hearing the fate of her people, she couldn't stay comfortable. God had work for her to do to fulfill her unique usefulness.

As we look at these facets of biblical justice, obeying and doing the good works God calls us to, we can have confidence that as the Holy Spirit works in us and through us, we will accomplish our unique usefulness by His power.

2. Generosity

Esther models generosity by the giving of her social resources, generously using her position as queen on behalf of the people.

To become generous like Esther, you and I need to recognize that all we have comes from God and belongs to God; we are simply stewards of our time, talent, social network, and finances. Our responsibility to God and our neighbor is to be generous with all we have to those in need.

Consider your social circles. Like Esther, how can you give generously with your "social resource" or influence?

____

____

____

____

In God's economy, in Proverbs 11:24–25 what does God say will be the results of our giving?

____

____

____

____

3. Equality

Equality in the time of Esther around 486–464 B.C. was defined by The Code of Hammurabi, written during the Babylonian time period somewhere between 1792–1750 BC. This was a set of 282 rules, governing commercial interactions, setting fines and punishments to meet the requirements of justice. Fines and punishments were based on class, not equality.[7]

"Biblical justice [on the other hand] requires every person to be treated according to the same standards and with the same respect, regardless of class, race, ethnicity, nationality, gender, or of any other social category"[8] (Leviticus 19:15; Deuteronomy 16:19; James 2:1–8). This is the equality that Esther was asking for: for her people to be given the same right to life as the Persians.

4. Advocacy:

In Esther 5, Esther advocates for her people. Esther may have heard growing up Psalm 41:1: ". . . Blessed are those who have regard for the weak; the LORD delivers them in times of trouble". The word translated "regard" means believers are to pay close attention to the weak and the poor, seeking to understand the causes of their condition, and to spend significant time and energy to change their life situation.[9]

The Jewish people were weak, unable to defend themselves against the king of Persia. The law written against them could not be reversed. They had no ability to raise themselves up from their situation.

But there was Esther. She had potential, privilege, and position. Esther used her social standing for the welfare of her people. She was the "other" Proverbs 31 woman: "Speak up for those who cannot speak for themselves . . . defend the rights of the poor and needy" (Proverbs 31:8–9).

God says all of His creation has the right to experience God's provision and that provision may need to come from the hands and generosity of you and me (Deuteronomy 24:17, 19).

Write down one person or group that like Esther, you could advocate for, support, or recommend on their behalf.

____

As we wrap up today, we see chapter 5 as the beginning of the turning point in our story. Esther, an obscure queen who would appear to have no power, exerts the power she does have, on behalf of God's people.

Here, through the grace extended to her by the king, we begin to see the shift, the reversal: God is on the move and His divine rescue and redemption are on the horizon. This shift from Esther being an observer to a difference-maker would never have been possible if the king had not extended to her the golden scepter.

You and I are not able to move from being a woman watching her world to a woman changing her world until we reach out and receive the power the Holy Spirit extends to us. Unless we receive the forgiveness of Christ and the power of the Holy Spirit, we will either sit in despair on our fallen planet, or we will work furiously as though we are the savior ourselves. When our unique usefulness is received and empowered by the Holy Spirit, we then partner with God and His gospel, the only power that will change our world.

As I have heard Amy say, "We don't have to do everything; just be faithful to our one thing." Ask the Lord: *What is my one thing?*

Pathway Principle

Moving from observer to difference-maker is only possible as we reach out and receive power from the Holy Spirit.

Memorize

"Dear friends, let us love one another, for love comes from God. Everyone who loves has been born of God and knows God. Whoever does not love does not know God, because God is love" (1 John 4:7–8).

Today, write out the memory verse four times and then read all four times aloud. Circle words that are meaningful to you.

Application

Choose one of the actions from Isaiah 58. Take some time to research ministries or organizations in your community that are taking responsibility to bring God's care to these people.

Day Three: The Wise Do It Slowly

I'm sorry to admit my own journey to "doing" began with less than pure motives.

My friend told me the Bible study I had written would be perfect for an organization in my community, Changed Choices, helping women build new lives after prison. I thought it would be a great opportunity to introduce my Bible study to a new audience.

Eager to learn more, I set a meeting with Gayle of Changed Choices with the goal of teaching these women and getting my Bible study in their hands.

But that is not what happened.

The organization didn't need a Bible study or a teacher. What they needed was for women to build friendships with women in prison and those coming out.

Just thinking about being in a setting outside my experience and education made my stomach feel a bit queasy. My gifts are in teaching and writing. I thought the opportunity was a bust.

After a few days of pondering the need that had been presented to me, I started thinking that this might just be God. So, with a heart filled with hesitation and a bit of doubt, I began learning what I didn't know, hoping to be used by the Lord even though I felt uncertain.

Me, a gal who knew nothing, dipping her toes into the world of incarceration, doing the work of advocacy. God used my not-so-pure motives to lead me into a new place of investing in the lives of these women. I began as a Bible study attendee, then a mentor, and today I lead the weekly Bible study. It was, and continues to be, a slow work. It isn't a work where I quickly see the fruits of the work being done. It is one lesson this speedster gal continues to learn, which is reinforced by Esther.

The wise do it slowly.

In Esther 5:6–8 (ESV), Esther didn't jump the first time the king asked, "What is your wish?" Instead, she calculated her move, inviting the king and Haman to a second banquet.

We understand why Esther invited the king, but why invite Haman?

Asking the one responsible for all this trouble seems unnecessary at the least and risky at most. When I am fearful and scared, or even irritated, I try to remove the source of my distress. Yet in her wisdom, Esther thinks of her community before she thinks of her comfort. Appealing to the king's desire to have his favorite at his side gains her even more favor.[10] She now has "the two most powerful men of the Persian empire, responding to her initiative."[11]

Why do you think Esther held two feasts? Why not make her request at the first one?

It makes me wonder. Commentaries are not in agreement as to why Esther held two banquets. Some think she may have lost her nerve. Others believe Esther was working to completely win the king over before she levied her big request, possibly using a delay tactic to heighten the king's interest.[12]

Whatever her core motivation, Esther slowed down, giving the entire process time to have its full work. In Esther 5:8 she said, "tomorrow I will do as the king has said" (ESV). Esther had the wisdom to know when to do what. Sometimes our action is immediate, sometimes there is a slight delay and many times, God asks us to wait.

Read James 1:1–8 in the King James Version. (You can find all translations on BibleGateway.com.) In verse 4, what trait does James say we should allow to have her perfect work in us?

Depending on the translation version you read personally, this verse may read: "let endurance have its perfect result" (AMP), "let steadfastness have its full effect" (ESV), or "let perseverance finish its work" (NIV). This passage, focusing on the work of trials in our lives, provides us the results that can come when we move slowly and don't rush the work God is doing in and through us.

Write below each noun listed in these various translations above. Now read them all in succession.

That is quite a list, isn't it?

James goes on to encourage us to ask for wisdom and expect God to deliver. Esther needed an exorbitant amount of wisdom and so do you and I as we become the hands and feet of Jesus in our communities.

Let's look at the second character in this chapter.

Read Esther 5:9–14. The first banquet is over and in a spectacular mood, Haman makes his way home. Suddenly, all that happiness drains out. What threw Haman into a tailspin?

What trait does Esther 5:10 say Haman showed?

Who even knows what fueled Haman's restraint? Based on his character, we cannot hope it was true self-control. Was he trying to keep it together and not draw attention to Mordecai defying him? Was he so mad he simply couldn't think of what to do next?

As the passage progresses, what causes Haman to throw off his restraint?

Haman gathers his family and friends for "show and tell." Remember in chapter 3 when we thought scripture hinted at Haman's insecurities? Chapter 5 verifies it. When a guy felt the need and "recounted to them the splendor of his riches, the number of his sons, all the promotions with which the king had honored him, and how he had advanced him above the officials and the servants of the king" (Esther 5:11 ESV). I see that level of bragging as a sure sign of insecurity. And Haman doesn't stop there! He goes on to say, "'And that's not all,' Haman added. 'I'm the only person Queen Esther invited to accompany the king to the banquet she gave. And she has invited me along with the king tomorrow'" (Esther 5:12). He sounds a lot like a middle school girl to me. I know in my own life, when I feel compelled to recount my achievements, I'm revealing my self-doubt.

Bible Nerd Box

Many translations in verse 11 use the word "boasted" to describe Haman's interaction with his family. Going back to the original Hebrew language, the word translated "recounted" in verse 11 in the ESV is a form of the verb *spr* in Hebrew. It means a missive, document, writing, or book.[13] It is as if Haman is reading what he's written, a documentation of why his life is valuable.

Haman's bragging reveals what he believes makes for a worthwhile life: money, recognition, and accumulation of things. He is telling those who *already know* about his wonderful life, another sure sign of insecurity. The irony is shortly none of these things will belong to Haman, and will in fact, be given to the very ones he despises (Esther 8:1–2; 9:25).

When I was trying to make the right decision about renewing the relationship with the boy-turned-man as I shared on day 1 of this week, I was so grateful to have in my life a wise counselor and friends who were also following Christ wholeheartedly. They helped me to make the right, although hard, decision.

In Haman's life, his wife and friends gave him a shove to leave self-control behind. He plunges headfirst into a solution to remove his misery: Have Mordecai murdered. "Only then can Haman's terrifying neediness be satisfied and his life of luxury begin again."[14] The scene is set; Haman is pleased. His obsession with his personal position and comfort will be his downfall.

How do our own positions and comforts keep us from doing what God wants us to do?

I know we don't like to look in a mirror and see the likeness of a Biblical villain, but can you, like me, see any of yourself in Haman? Sometimes when I'm making a decision, I unconsciously look for those who will agree with me and the way I see things. It feels like Haman has done the same.

He attempts to push away his problem by surrounding himself with friends and family who see things the way he does. They tell him exactly what he wants to hear: Fix it! Don't just wait for the edict for the annihilation of the Jews. Move![15]

This is all it takes for Haman to forego his fetters; the gallows for Mordecai's demise are created. Adding to the many ironies in this story, Haman's demand to relieve his present pain will be the very tool used to permanently relieve his pain via his own death.

Can you think of a time in your life when your rush to relieve your pain only brought on more?

The chapter ends with Haman implementing his own good idea. What you and I know is that while it is a detestable plan, God will still use it. God is working invisibly and behind the scenes.

Pathway Principle

As we move to do the work God calls us to, we can trust that no matter how things may appear, God is at work behind the scenes.

Memorize

Today, fill in the blanks. Once you're finished, read it aloud once while clapping your hands in rhythm.

"Dear friends, let us ______ ______ ______, for love comes from God. Everyone who loves has been ____ ___ ___ and knows God. Whoever ______ ______ love does not ______ ______, because God is ______" (1 John 4:7–8).

Application

As you have been praying and seeking God about your own unique usefulness, is there something happening that feels detrimental to your next step? Write out a time in your past, when you were also facing something negative, and God turned it around for His glory and your good. Thank the Lord for this remembrance and praise Him that you will see His faithfulness again!

Day Four: As Two People Prepare

When Esther 4 ended, we saw Esther inform Mordecai that she and her young women were going to prepare for her next move by fasting. She is now taking charge and making the call of what to do. Up until now,

Esther had solely taken instruction from others. Now she is making decisions. She asked Mordecai to ask all the Jews in Susa to join them in the fast. Esther recognized her need for spiritual preparation before she headed into a situation that would yield either very positive, or very negative, results. Fasting was the "organized activity aimed at increasing Esther's chances of success, through earnest prayer—the strongest indication yet of Esther's (and Mordecai's) faith in God."[16] Unsure of her outcome, yet sure of the possibility of trouble as well as her obedience, Esther did what she could to prepare spiritually beforehand.

In Esther 5:8, Esther was heading off to prepare for the second feast. The whole point of these feasts was to circumvent the original evil plan of Haman. What Esther didn't know was there was even more evil at work than she was aware of.

As you and I move into our own unique usefulness in God's kingdom, the same is true for us. While we are making our plans to do good works for our King, we need to know that the entire time, the enemy is making his own plan to stop God by stopping us.

In the book of Ephesians, the apostle Paul's letter to the people of God in Ephesus, Paul instructs this New Testament church on how to prepare spiritually for the trials and troubles they face each day as followers of Christ. The Ephesians were living each day in a city known for its "fascination with magic and the occult."[17] Demonic influence was no small matter in this city with a long history of being under the control of hell's power and darkness. Acts 19:19 tells of Ephesians coming to faith in Jesus: "A number of them who had been practicing sorcery brought their incantation books and burned them at a public bonfire. The value of the books was several million dollars" (NLT).

In Ephesians 6:10–19, Paul instructs these new followers of Jesus to protect themselves from this evil power. To communicate this concept, Paul uses imagery familiar to those under Rome's rule: a soldier's armor.

Like Esther in Persia and the Ephesians in Paul's time, you and I also face spiritual resistance to God and His will being accomplished. This resistance is sometimes called spiritual warfare. Let's look at how

Paul tells you and I to prepare for this resistance and "the schemes of the devil" (Ephesians 6:11 ESV).

Read Ephesians 6:10–19. As you read, write each weapon under either Offensive or Defensive based on its uses below.

Offensive	Defensive
______________	______________
______________	______________
______________	______________
______________	______________
______________	______________

Describe each weapon you list. (Words given in the passage may be useful.)

____

____

____

____

____

____

Preparation for "doing" in the kingdom of God begins first with preparation spiritually, and then it moves into preparing practically.

As I reread Esther 5 it struck me: Two people were preparing two opposing events at the same time.

In Esther 5:4 and 5:8, Esther speaks of preparing for a feast. What type of work goes into preparing for a feast?

____

____

____

____

____

I know that may have seemed like an obvious exercise, but I want us to recognize that doing God's work sometimes involves physical work. Someone had to prepare the food, set the table, pour the wine. Esther uses the words "I will prepare" in Esther 5:8. As queen, I'm not sure how many pots and pans she would have dirtied, but there was work she would have done to see that the banquet was ready. Maybe she inspected the produce, placed the meat order, tasted the wine, or chose the entertainment.

At Changed Choices, my current role is teaching Bible study each week. My work is *also* to take my turn bringing a meal, helping to clean up the dishes, and helping provide transportation for our clients. This physical work is also part of my doing good works and fulfilling my unique usefulness. God's work includes both the things we think of as spiritual work—praying, fasting, teaching—and the dirty work that we often want to relegate to someone else.

Can you name some opportunities you might have in your community involving various kinds of work?

____

____

____

____

There are some folks who look down on the more practical side of doing ministry or good works. They want the "flashy," the famous side. In fact, 53 percent of Americans say they would like to be at least slightly famous.[18] With fame getting all the fanfare, we elevate the "shiny" and can look down on the serving. It appears we have lost our appreciation for work. Or sometimes we try to make our work flashy to point to ourselves. We have to be very careful of our motives.

After serving at Changed Choices for a few months, my friend was finally coming home from prison, and I was ecstatic to welcome her! Making my homemade cheesecake and picking up some flowers from the store, I waited, somewhat impatiently, for her arrival at the Changed Choices transition home. The day was more than I could have hoped for! We ate dessert, went out to lunch, and then unpacked the few things she had. That evening, I did something I rarely do regarding our organization. I posted a picture of the two of us on my social media, sharing my excitement.

The next day I received a text from a woman I highly respect, who had at one point been a part of the Changed Choices staff. With the utmost kindness, she shared with me why my post was not the good thing I had hoped. "When you tell their story, it makes them feel tokenized. Because they need help, they often fear saying anything. Any act of kindness including you taking a cake and flowers is such a sweet gesture, which I know comes from a good place. But when the person giving makes it public, clients often wonder if it's for them or not. Trust is hard for them, and there's often shame at being in prison and needing help. They can wonder: *Is what is being done really about me?* Trust is hard for them. If a close friend, like Amy, did something and went to jail, what would you do and what would you post?"

In Psalm 90:17, what prayer is prayed concerning our work?

When our doing involves the practicality of giving, what instructions does Matthew 6:3 give us?

It seems we are back at week 1 with our motivation again. I think this just shows how this process of listen, feel, do, and speak is not all linear, but more circular.

As we move from listening and feeling and into the actual doing of good works, you and I need to continually keep our hearts in check, as well as continue to listen to those who know more than us in the area we are working.

My wise advisor was right, my heart only wanted to celebrate with my friend's release from incarceration. But out of a place of wanting to exercise wisdom, I took the post down, but continued to celebrate in the heart the good things God had done.

Pathway Principle

While we are making our plans to do good works for our King, we need to know that the entire time, the enemy is making his own plan to stop God by stopping us.

Memorize

Today, fill in the blanks. Once you're finished, read it aloud once while clapping your hands in rhythm.

"Dear friends, let us ______ ______ ______, for love comes from God. Everyone who loves has been _____ ____ ____ and knows God. Whoever ____ ______ ______does not know God, because God is love" (1 John 4:7–8).

Now try to say it aloud without looking. Don't worry about mistakes. Just use it as an opportunity to see what your brain hasn't "caught" yet. Read the sections aloud that you had trouble with several more times.

Application

As you have stepped forward into doing good works, how have you experienced resistance? Before this week, had you recognized this as the work of the enemy against the plans of God?

Day Five: Don't Doubt What God Is Doing That You Cannot See

From our vantage point, we can see as the story progresses, that even as things were heating up against her, God would reverse the entire plan. Isaiah 54:17 would come true: "'no weapon forged against you will prevail, and you will refute every tongue that accuses you. This is the heritage of the servants of the Lord, and this is their vindication from me,' declares the Lord."

The whole chapter of Esther 6 could appear to be a series of "just so happens to be" moments. But you and I know, it is really God at work.

Read Esther 6, listing the "just so happens to be" moments you spot.

No matter what we've been taught, there really is no such thing as coincidence.

God uses the details of His doing and our doing to shape His story.

What is your favorite type of story or movie? Esther contains many elements of great storytelling, like these unpredictable moments, while also being "the most ironically comic scene in the entire Bible."[19]

In order to make full sense of this chapter, let's revisit Mordecai in chapter 2.

Reread Esther 2:19–23. How do things end for Mordecai in the last verse of the chapter?

Five years have gone by since Mordecai uncovered the conspiracy against the king, but Mordecai has yet to be recognized for his good work (cf. 2:16; 3:7). Typically, Persian kings publicly rewarded those who demonstrated their loyalty. By doing so, they promoted to their other citizens that it was worthwhile to protect their king. It would have been natural for Mordecai to expect recognition.[20]

When have you done something good, and it was overlooked?

What happened next in Esther 3:1?

What feelings might this action have produced in Mordecai?

I wonder if Mordecai thought "What's up with that, God?" when he wasn't rewarded for his good work. Did he struggle to continue in his service to the king when it went unnoticed and felt like it got him nowhere?

Whether we're looking at Mordecai's life or our own, God's timing can seem tricky, can't it? We can be doing everything we know that's pleasing to God and yet not see the evidence of His pleasure in our lives. At least not yet.

When we are in this space of doing good works with God and we do not see the results we anticipated or the outcome we expected, our eyes and heart can wander toward doubt. It's easy to slip into spotlighting the outcomes and results others are experiencing in their work with God. The enemy contrives his derailing trick: Look away from God's commission for me comparing it to God's calling for you.

Henri J.M. Nouwen, a Dutch Catholic priest, professor, writer, and theologian said: "You have to start trusting your unique vocation and allow it to grow deeper and stronger in you so it can blossom in your community." Nouwen really encouraged me to desire this mark of spiritual maturity: "You will be able to understand and appreciate [the value of other people's spiritual experience] without desiring to imitate them. You will be more self-confident and free to claim your unique place in life as God's gift to you."[21]

It sure appears this was where Mordecai was at. Karen Jobes writes: "Mordecai had no doubt been keenly disappointed by this oversight. His willingness to overlook the slight and continue faithfully to serve the king gives insight into his character."[22] When not acknowledged for his good work, we don't see Mordecai back up or quit in his service. He continues to do the good and right thing, even while he is not appreciated or applauded. Maybe he looked to Joseph as his example of continuing to do good and right, even when it was not rewarded. (Carve out some time to read Genesis 37–44, and read Joseph's response when he was not rewarded.)

In Esther 6:10, when his reward finally comes, Mordecai is right where he's always been, doing his duty. "The king told Haman, 'Hurry, and do just as you proposed. Take a garment and a horse for Mordecai the Jew, who is sitting at the King's Gate. Do not leave out anything you have suggested" (CSB).

After Mordecai saved the king's life in Esther 2 and received no acknowledgement and at the end of Esther 6 after receiving much affirmation, Mordecai appears to simply go back to work.

How does Colossians 3:23–24 tell us to do our work?

____

____

____

____

How would you describe the word "whatever" as used in Colossians 3:23?

____

____

____

____

Dictionary.com says it means: anything that, no matter what.[23]

We are to work, in everything we do, with heart for the Lord. In the original Greek language the New Testament was written in, *with all our heart* means with all our psyche; our life, soul, heart, and mind. This verse is very convicting for a box-checker like me. God addresses not just our actions, but our motives. Doing whatever I do, heartily and for the Lord, may not be easy, but keeping in mind that God is my rewarder will empower me.

Here in the last few chapters of Esther, God was certainly at work, which will be so boldly seen as these next chapters unfold.

Think of the last movie you saw where you were on the edge of your seat. Was the heroine on the verge of death? Were the lovers being torn apart, to be separated forever?

In most stories, the climax involves high action. The pivoting point of this story, however, is not where you would think it would be. The turning point in Esther begins with a king's sleepless night.

In chapter 6, what did Esther and Mordecai do to contribute to Mordecai being honored by the king?

What part did Esther and Mordecai play in this beginning of God's divine series of reversals?

Here is the beginning of the series of great reversals for Mordecai, Esther, and the entire Jewish people. As always, God has a purpose for His plan. "By making the pivot point . . . an insignificant event rather than the point of highest dramatic tension, the author is taking the focus away from human action."[24] This helps show that, although Mordecai and Esther are at work in this situation, the outcome of the book is not simply a reward for their labors. "They do not 'cause' the victory—they are, indeed, barely involved in this chapter."[25]

Had the turning point been Esther's approaching the king uninvited or when she confronted Haman on his wicked plot, Esther would have been in the spotlight. Esther would have received the glory for beginning the reversals. But it does not. Without using God's name, the author reveals humans are not the heroes of this story.

Nor are we to be the heroes of ours. Every piece of our stories, our lives, God is using and redeeming, to glorify Himself. And as in the story of Esther, our God cannot be explained nor can anyone or anything stop Him. He is controlling the end of Esther's story, writing history to demonstrate His continued faithfulness to the Israelite people.

He is writing our stories as well. I've had a year of sleepless nights. While I'm not aware of how God might be using them, who knows if the prayers I've prayed on those restless nights have not been ordained by Him? Who knows if the work I am doing, praying instead of sleeping, is not in fact changing the trajectory of the future of the very one I am praying for?

Who is to say when you turned the channel from the show not glorifying God, you stood up for a defenseless child, or carried the groceries for the elderly woman, you were, in fact, a divine intersection by God to show Him to another?

God can and does use the big and *the small*, often turning our small into something bigger, using ordinary life events like sleepless nights, to make His name famous as well.

When has a seemingly insignificant event in your life led to something life changing? Think of how you came to know the Lord, met your spouse, got your job, moved into your home, chose your church, or attended a school.

Just reading Esther 6 can reassure you and me, that no matter how things appear, no matter how much time has passed and how forgotten and discouraged you may feel, God can do anything! He can take the worst possible situation and completely turn it around, if that is in fact, what He wills to do.

Jesus stated His will plain and simple: "'For I have come down from heaven, not to do my own will but the will of him who sent me'" John

6:38 (ESV). That will, from birth to death, was to point and glorify Himself through the redeeming work of the cross.

"The cross of Jesus Christ is the pivot point of the great reversal of history, where our sorrow has been turned to joy."[26] This is not to say that God, while we are on this earth, will turn every experience of conflict and trial out the way we want and hope. But we do know that one day, for those of us who have asked for His forgiveness and made Him our Lord, "He will wipe away every tear from their eyes, and death shall be no more, neither shall there be mourning, nor crying, nor pain anymore, for the former things have passed away" (Revelation 21:4 ESV).

Pathway Principle

God uses the details of our doing and His to shape His story for His glory.

Memorize

"Dear friends, let us ______ ______ ______, for love comes from God. Everyone who loves has been ____ ___ ___ and knows God. Whoever ____ _____ ______ does not know God, because God is love" (1 John 4:7–8).

Today, cover our memory verse with your hand and repeat it four times. It's ok if you have to peek if you need to!

Application

Thank the Lord for the past "just so happens" moments in your life when He was at work. Be on the lookout for these types of scenarios in your future, thanking Him for being at work as they come along.

Do Pathway Principles

We can choose what is right not knowing if it will turn out right.

Moving from observer to difference-maker is only possible as we reach out and receive power from the Holy Spirit.

As we move to do the work God calls us to, we can trust that no matter how things may appear, God is at work behind the scenes.

While we are making our plans to do good works for our King, we need to know that the entire time, the enemy is making his own plan to stop God by stopping us.

God uses the details of our doing and His to shape His story for His glory.

Prayer

Spirit of the Living God, whatever You are calling me to do, be it small or big, may I always see it is Your doing and turn the spotlight forever on You. In Jesus' name, Amen.

Questions for Discussion or Personal Journaling

1. When have you been in the crux between doing what is right and a potentially scary outcome?

2. What did you learn as you studied Esther 5 and 6 this week?

3. How does Ephesians 2:10 speak to you, "For we are God's handiwork, created in Christ Jesus to do good works, which God prepared in advance for us to do"?

4. Read this week's memory verse: "Beloved, let us love one another, for love is from God, and whoever loves has been born of God and knows God. Anyone who does not love does not know God, because God is love" (1 John 4:7–8 ESV). What connection is there between loving God, loving others, and doing good works?

5. When you read Deuteronomy 10:17–19, which action listed pulls on your heart more than another? Does a next step come to mind for you?

6. As you have prayed and asked the Lord, *What is my one thing?*, has anything begun to emerge?

7. How do our own positions and comfort keep us from doing what God wants us to do?

8. Read Ephesians 6:10–19. Lynn said on day 4, "While we are making our plans to do good works for our King, we need to know that the entire time, the enemy is making his own plan to stop God by stopping us." As you have stepped forward into doing good works, how have you experienced resistance? Before this week, had you recognized this as the work of the enemy against the plans of God?

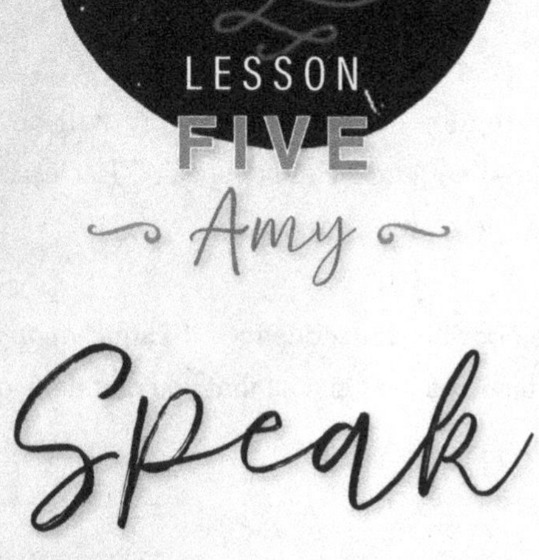

Day One: Time to Speak Up

Maybe you've gotten to know me well enough by now that you're seeing what's happening. This study of Esther came about because of my friend Lynn's astute insight during her personal Bible study time. For years, I'd been personally moving through a process that I believed that God gave me—just me—to listen, feel, do, and *then* speak. It was a painful process for this word-y girl to speak last, so I had been processing it with my friends Lynn and Suzie. Yes, you can read either processing or whining. There was quite a bit of both.

One day, Lynn reached out to me with excitement. "Amy!" she exclaimed. "Your process isn't just for you at all! God gave it to Esther first. I saw it in my personal study, and now I'm seeing the pattern with lots of people He used in the Bible."

That was a moment for me. Instead of feeling so alone with my struggle to learn and grow in this new process, I realized that I was truly surrounded by "such a great cloud of witnesses" (Hebrews 12:1). If you're starting to realize this process is for you, too, not just Esther and me, hop on the struggle bus!

This week we're going to tackle the last step of the process to become part of God's big story. As Lynn mentioned, this process is circular, so we'll have lots of opportunity to practice. Hallelujah! Honestly, this has been the hardest step for me, and it probably will be for you too. But there's "a time to be silent and a time to speak" (Ecclesiastes 3:7), and this is Esther's time to speak. It's ours, too.

What were the possible consequences if Esther *hadn't* used words and spoken at the time she did? List all that you can think of that would have been lost.

Read Esther 7 two times. We're going to read our chapters over and over again this week, mining out each shining nugget! Record your thoughts and observations here, truths that the Holy Spirit made stand out to you.

Consider these questions as you raise the Bible-study bar for yourself:

- What's a fresh insight you have on this chapter in light of your previous weeks of study?

→ What are you seeing differently now?

____

____

____

____

____

____

→ How do you see Esther growing and changing?

____

____

____

____

____

____

→ What new personal insights do you have from reading this chapter?

____

____

____

____

____

As a woman who loves words herself, this chapter in the book of Esther sets my soul on fire. Esther's words are her God-given weapon. Without donning armor or swinging a sword, she uses words well to persuade power, score a crushing blow against God's enemies, and save her people.

Our God, who describes Himself as the Word in John 1, imbues words with power that we often underestimate. Let's put Esther's use of words under the microscope so that we can be like her, women who speak up to make a difference for God in our world. Let's learn to use our words as agents of God's redemption.

Let's play "This or That." Circle the adjectives describing Esther's request to the king in verses 3–4.

This	or	That
Fuzzy		Clear
Humble		Arrogant
Demanding		Courteous
General		Specific
Kind		Brash
Respectful		Harsh
Reckless		Measured
Thought-out		Spontaneous

When Esther finally delivered her request to the king, she used words in a powerful but winsome way. For me, that feels like a very important lesson as we navigate speaking up into our divided world in godly ways.

Proverbs is a book of the Bible that's full of good advice about how to speak up. Let's look at just a handful of verses today. I encourage you, however, to put further study of Proverbs on your to-do list with the goal of learning how to speak up well.

Read these instructions from Proverbs and record the lesson you learned.

Proverbs 8:6–7

Proverbs 10:19 (Note: I might need to get this one tattooed someplace where I can always see it!)

Proverbs 16:13

Proverbs 16:24

Proverbs 17:27

**Our words are to be wise, not wasteful.
Our words are to be kind, not soul-killers.
Our words are to be righteous,
not random or reckless.**

Being people who speak up, like Esther in this passage, doesn't mean we just let words fly from our mouth or flow from our fingers onto a keyboard. It's not "speaking your mind," "telling it how you see it," or "just telling the 'truth'" (which is only our opinion).

Being a godly person who speaks up in godly ways means we are Holy Spirit–led. We speak words of truth, wisdom, and honor. We are "quick to listen, slow to speak" (James 1:19). Our words are to be beautiful and helpful to others, like "apples of gold in settings of silver" (Proverbs 25:11), even when they're hard to hear. All of our words are infused with love so they don't become "a resounding gong or a clanging cymbal" (1 Corinthians 13:1).

Even though it's uncomfortable to speak up, there's a time when God calls us to wrap words around His ways.

The people God created are still in pain and crisis all over the world. There's poverty, human trafficking, gender inequality, refugees, racism, homelessness, mental illness, hunger, disease, violence, abuse, mass incarceration . . . the list of this world's evils and the ravages they inflict on humanity could go on and on. We know these aren't just "out there." This is pain being suffered by those in our communities. Our neighborhoods.

Let's not make the mistake of abusing grace, trusting God's sovereignty to the exclusion of our own action. Counselors Bill and Kristi Gualtiere say it this way, "If we're not careful we can get *paralyzed by grace.* In this case we misrepresent God's sovereignty and grace so that our free choice and personal responsibility are diminished. We tell ourselves it's all up to the omni-Lord who gets saved or healed or helped and how things work out in our world, so we feel no urgency to do the work of God's kingdom."[1]

God is calling you into His story. You and I are His agents for His redemption in other's lives.

Set a timer for five minutes. Sit in stillness and silence with an open heart, giving the Holy Spirit space to speak. Ask God if He wants to use You to ease the crisis of His people in some way. When you're done, write down what you believe to be your unique usefulness.

When Silence Switches

When I was a girl, especially in middle school and early in high school, I was incredibly opinionated and loved the sound of every opinion that spilled out of my mouth. I craved a debate, and I relished *crushing* you in a war of words.

Then something life-altering happened to me. At sixteen, I stalked a boy to a Bible study. That's right. God will use any means to get you where He wants you. He leveraged my crush on a guy to lead me to a place with people who were different from anyone I had ever known. There was a revival sweeping the teenagers in my town, and it was led by people who had made Jesus everything.

I had never experienced Jesus that way. Suddenly, I wanted what they had. My crush faded while my passion for Jesus grew, and I've never been the same.

One transformation God orchestrated during that time was the shutting of my mouth. As He taught me His higher ways and higher thoughts in Scripture, I realized that my opinion was worth . . . well, the proverbial two cents. Learning to value God's Word over my own words was a necessary but painful dying-to-self process.

Choosing silence was an act of obedience at that point, and God called it good!

Years later, silence became something else entirely. Instead of choosing silence to learn more about God, I started choosing silence in crisis to:

Fit in.
Get along.
Appear righteous.
Fit the acceptable mold for a Christian woman.
Protect my reputation.

And even though it may have appeared virtuous, my silence was motivated by fear and people-pleasing.

I realized my silence had gone from being truly righteous to outright disobedient. I had let the silence stretch too long, letting self-protection be my motive for silence not righteousness. There were things I *should* have been speaking up about. God shone His light on my heart and showed me it needed work, but He had a purpose for my voice. Self-protective silence wasn't an option anymore. It had become sinful behavior.

Is any of my story similar to yours? Are you still in the righteous silence—the kind that is essential while you're listening, feeling, and doing—or have you moved into sinful silence? Take a moment to sit quietly, listening for the Holy Spirit. Is there something for which you need to confess to God and ask forgiveness? Or something else the Spirit reveals that's hiding in your heart? Record it here.

What might be the consequences of continuing in sinful silence (remember, that's different from righteous silence)? List all the opportunities that you can think of that will be lost, missed, or postponed if you don't use your voice for your unique usefulness.

I'm not going to lie. This new season in my life of speaking up has been one of the most difficult seasons I've ever lived. I've had to face the pain of personal failure and nurse wounds inflicted by those who disagree with me. But there have been sweet things, too. I've lost followers, but I've gained friends, true sisters who are walking with me, like Lynn and this blog-reader, Michele O'Leary who said:

"Amy, I have been stalking you as you journey deeper and deeper in the call that God has placed on your heart. You are helping me tip toe, with a tender heart and strong voice, forward in my own Holy Spirit convictions. I am in the listening and learning stage, as I take classes, read books, listen to podcasts and so forth. Cheering you on. I am grateful for folks who are steps ahead of me to help me learn, then I pass it on."[2]

When we speak up, we will lose some things, but what we gain is so much richer. Just like Esther, we gain God's pleasure. We may never have a book written about us, but we'll have the joy of being close to His heart.

And we'll gain a community of others who are using their voice to bring redemption into their unique usefulness. This is a circle of friends like none other, bound by the battles we've fought together.

If you choose silence and your voice is lost, who knows what redemption has been lost. Let's choose to be godly people speaking up in godly ways instead!

Pathway Principle

Godly people speak up in godly ways.

Memorize

"She speaks with wisdom, and faithful instruction is on her tongue" (Proverbs 31:26).

Read the memory verse aloud four times. Read it very slowly the first time and faster each subsequent time.

Application

What "platforms" has God given you where it may be time to speak up? For example: your dinner table, your homeowner's association meeting, your family reunion, your workplace, your social media account, across the table at the coffee shop, in a mentoring relationship, in your home with your children . . .

Day Two: Speak Up for Life

I have a confession. As a fifty-three-year-old woman, I exchanged my ancient license plate for my first vanity plate last year. You know the license plates that have a message embedded in them? I blush because I understand that *vanity* might be the key word, but I just couldn't resist. After years of speaking and writing, I gave myself a title that labels the back of my car: WORD GRL.

I've always generated a lot of words. I was the little girl that the teacher constantly moved around the room in an effort to stop my chatting with my neighbors. (She couldn't find a soul I wouldn't talk to.) As a communicator by trade, I value words even more than before, and I love when a new word wraps around an idea in a way that brings clarity. Words have power. Scripture confirms this in Proverbs 18:21 where it says, "The tongue has the power of life and death, and those who love it will eat its fruit."

I can't think of anyone who must have felt the weight of her words more heavily than Esther. From his past performances, her husband, the King, had proven that her next words could save her or slay her. Let's read them together.

Reread Esther 7:3–4 and then fill in the blanks with one key word:

"Then Queen Esther answered, 'If I have found favor with you, Your Majesty, and if it pleases you, grant me my ___________—this is my petition. And spare my people—this is my request.'"

Finally, Esther had reached the turning point. In it, she spoke up, asking for her own _________ and the_____________ of her people.

Esther's unique usefulness was to be the intermediary who spoke up for and protected life. She even confessed to the king that she wouldn't have come to him for anything less, even if she and her people were to be enslaved.

In speaking up, Esther knew she was requesting physical life. She may not have understood she was also ensuring the nation of Israel would fulfill its plan, producing a Savoir who gave spiritual and eternal life. God cares deeply about both.

Speaking Up for Physical Life

Esther and her people were standing on the precipice of extinction. Their lives were facing a clear and present danger as the edict had called for them to be destroyed, killed, and annihilated—every last man, woman and child (Esther 3:13). Their goods were to be plundered. They were about to lose life, living, and home. Haman essentially had commanded that the Jews be erased.

I've called Esther a reluctant advocate, but she was also the *sole* advocate, the only one in place who could rescue these threatened lives. She held a place of privilege and power, but instead of using it like the king to protect her pleasures, Esther was being asked to speak up to protect others with her privileges. It's an echo of the way another woman, a mother, used her own voice to influence her son, the king.

Read Proverbs 31:1–9. What pleasures is this mother warning the king about?

In verses 8–9, how does she urge him to invest his life, power, and voice?

Who are to be the recipients of his advocacy and protection?

Since King Solomon, the richest king of Israel, wrote the rest of the book of Proverbs, most scholars agree this passage is written by him also about the teachings of his mother, Bathsheba. (That's its own glimpse at a redemption story, isn't it?) If you're holding this book in your hand, you are likely one of the world's privileged. Like mine, your bank balance probably doesn't come anywhere close to King Solomon's, but let's put things into perspective.

In 2017, with over 689 million people in the world, 9.2 percent of the world's population lived in extreme poverty, making less than two dollars per day. Roughly 24.1 percent (almost one in four people in the world) subsisted on around three dollars per day and 43.3 percent on $5.50 per day.[3]

Those are staggering numbers. The 2020 pandemic made everything far bleaker. Day laborers, making barely enough each day to survive, weren't able to work at all during the pandemic lockdowns. The numbers of people in poverty soared, and experts say hundreds of millions of people were pushed into extreme poverty, ending the upward trend of income. It sent impoverished people into a backward spiral that set our world back decades. These are people, like the Jews in Persia during Esther's time, with no voice or power.

Big numbers are overwhelming and often unimaginable, so let's pause here for a moment. I want to take you into the tiny one-room house I visited in India several years ago where a young mother was barely surviving with her two young children. A lockdown would mean no day labor. No day labor means no food. No food means increased vulnerability to disease. Poverty, starvation, disease, and despair might well lead this mother from dignified household work to selling her body as a living. This isn't an exaggerated story. This would be a reality for that young mother, and it is a reality for many in some parts of our world.

More than ever in our own lifetime, the physical bodies of many in our world are at risk, and we are those with the privilege and power to step up and speak out for rescue. We are called to fulfill Isaiah 1:17 in our day, "Learn to do right; seek justice. Defend the oppressed. Take up the cause of the fatherless; plead the case of the widow."

Prayerfully read over this list and circle one or two that move your heart toward action:

- Research how to receive prayer requests from an aide organization.
- Research relief organizations and give to one doing good work.
- Volunteer at your local food bank.
- Donate to your local food bank.
- Write a letter to a government leader supporting legislation that helps the poor.
- Speak up in your social media and in conversations to build awareness and be an advocate for the poor.
- Create a fundraiser to build community and help the poor at the same time.
- Organize a fun event with the proceeds being given to a relief organization.
- Other: ________________________________

I hope you see what I've done here. Being an advocate for the poor isn't a one-size-fits-all proposition. Some of us don't like to verbalize as much as others. If you're in that camp, there are options for you, too! We can speak up for the poor and oppressed, those who are voiceless and powerless, in many different ways. By activating our gifts, resources, and time, we can save physical lives through our unique usefulness just like Esther did.

Speaking Up for Spiritual Life

Generations before Jesus was born, God used Esther as an agent of rescue for Jesus' lineage. Esther helped ensure the life of the one who is Life.

Match the Scripture to the truth about Jesus. Jesus is:

The Author of life	John 1:4
The life and light of man	John 6:35
The resurrection and the life	John 11:25
The way and the truth and the life	John 14:6
The bread of life	Acts 3:14–15

Truly, if you do extended study, you can fill months doing a New Testament word search for the word "life." (And that's what we word-girls geek out on, right? Add it to your study list!)

Jesus Himself is life, and He gives us new life.

Jesus gave us two clear steps to gain this new life. Fill in the two words that tell us how we receive new life through Christ.

"The time has come," he said. "The kingdom of God has come near. ____________ and ____________ the good news" (Mark 1:15)!

Anyone who repents, asking forgiveness and turning away from sin, and believes that Jesus is the Savior receives eternal spiritual life through Him. This is the deeper life that we all long for, and it all comes through Jesus.

Jesus not only gives us life. Remember when we defined the word "advocate" in week 3? Scripture tells us that He is the advocate for us and all who we lead to Him. First John 2:1b says, "But if anybody does sin, we have an advocate with the Father—Jesus Christ, the Righteous One." Jesus sits at the right hand of His Father advocating for us (Romans 8:34), using His words to ensure eternal life for us. I'm undone just typing these powerful truths.

But as moved as I feel about Jesus' advocacy for me, I have to admit

I haven't always applied that same passion to telling others about the new life in Jesus that's available to them. My heart is pierced thinking of opportunities I've allowed to pass without speaking.

Esther spoke up, securing life for herself and her people. She was an agent of rescue for physical lives, but she also protected the line of the coming Savior, the one who would pay with His physical life for our spiritual life. We're now called to speak up in the same way. Yes, saving physical lives is important and God-ordained work, but the saving of spiritual lives requires speaking, too. As Romans 10:17 tells us, good deeds fall short of what's needed, "Consequently, faith comes from hearing the message, and the message is heard through the word about Christ."

Spend a moment in silence, listening, asking the Holy Spirit for opportunities to speak about Jesus' offer of life. Circle people below who God prompts you to pray for who need to receive eternal life. Pray for opportunities to share the Good News of Jesus with them.

My neighbor	My friend
My spouse	My extended family
My coworker	A familiar stranger
My child	Other__________(like the cashier at your grocery store)

Lynn's going to give us some warnings next week about tying our stories too closely to Esther's, but at this point in the story, we can choose her as our role model. Let's decide right here and now to speak up for life!

Pathway Principle

Godly people speak up for both spiritual and physical life.

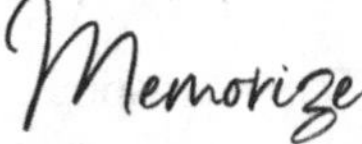

"She speaks with wisdom, and faithful instruction is on her tongue" (Proverbs 31:26).

Today, write out the memory verse four times and then read all four times aloud. Circle words that are meaningful to you.

Application

Go back to the list where you circled ways that you can help to save physical bodies. Write one action step on your calendar to complete this week either to volunteer or give.

Go back to the list where you circled people with whom God is calling you to share Jesus' life. Write one action step on your calendar to pray or serve.

Note: In this week, I mentioned my trip to India. One of my favorite global organizations that does literacy and relief work in India is Mission India. Visit their website today to find small and large ways to help. I love getting their daily prayer requests in my email! See https://missionindia.org.

Day Three: Speak Up Against Evil

Through sobs so deep that I could barely understand her, my friend gulped out her heart-breaking story. Her pastor had silenced her with harsh, cutting words about her that I knew to be untrue to the core. After being questioned about deceitful behavior in church policies, he had shut her down so that he could shut her up. I took a deep breath and then spoke words that I knew might be met with resistance. "First, we need to put the appropriate label on what just happened. *That* was spiritual abuse." *Spiritual abuse* is defined as "any attempt to exert power and control over someone using religion, faith, or beliefs."[4]

As a culture, we've become reluctant to call evil what it is. We're hesitant to call out sin and put the correct label on it. Esther didn't shrink back.

Read Esther 7:5–10. What words did Esther use to describe Haman in verse 6?

____

____

____

____

____

What do you think? Were those the correct labels to put on Haman? Why or why not? How might you have labeled Haman?

____

____

____

____

____

Haman's plan was evil, and we see sinfulness in his actions. In the review verses below, put a word or phrase beside each to identify and label the action appropriately with the sin(s) it displays.

__________ Esther 3:5, "When Haman saw that Mordecai would not kneel down or pay him honor, he was enraged."

__________ Esther 3:6b, "Haman looked for a way to destroy all Mordecai's people, the Jews, throughout the whole kingdom of Xerxes."

_______________ Esther 3:15, "The couriers went out, spurred on by the king's command, and the edict was issued in the citadel of Susa. The king and Haman sat down to drink, but the city of Susa was bewildered."

_______________ Esther 5:9, "But when he saw Mordecai at the king's gate and observed that he neither rose nor showed fear in his presence, he was filled with rage against Mordecai."

_______________ Esther 5:11, "Haman boasted to them about his vast wealth, his many sons, and all the ways the king had honored him and how he had elevated him above the other nobles and officials."

Haman was an evil man who manifested evil acts in layers of sin, and Esther was right to call him out.

Turn. Turn. Turn.

Bible Nerd Box

It's interesting to note that the Hebrew words used by both the king and Esther in verses 5–6 sound harsh and sharp in the original spoken language. Here's the sign of another effective storytelling tool used by the unknown writer of Esther. The author used speech-like sound effects!

Esther is a book *full* of plot twists and reversals. One commentator uses the literary term *peripety*, a sudden turn of events, to identify God's providential actions in Esther. When Haman had to lead Mordecai on the horse around town, that honor that Haman craved, that was one of the first peripeties in Esther's story. This scene, where Esther exposes Haman, the tide turns in an enormous wave against him. It's a major peripety in the book. There's another event in Scripture with a peripety that we need to examine to understand the role of speaking up in identifying evil.

Read Genesis 11:1–9. How many languages were there in the whole world at the beginning of the story?

What was the unified goal of the people in verse 4?

In Exodus 20:3, God says, "You shall have no other gods before me." In light of this command, why was the people's goal evil?

What was God's action to prevent this evil from occurring?

In the story of Babel, the people tried to use their common language as a means to unify themselves. They wanted to be as powerful as God. In a providential peripety, God confused their speech, thus creating many languages so this evil goal couldn't be met.

And yet, God has used our speech to restore and redeem ever since. God made it clear in the story of Babel that collective speech is designed by Him to be used for His glory alone. In her speech, Esther called life good and destruction evil. When we do the same, we give God glory.

Yet, we live in a world that Isaiah describes well when he said, "Woe to those who call evil good and good evil, who put darkness for light and light for darkness, who put bitter for sweet and sweet for bitter" (Isaiah 5:20). As Isaiah states, humanity and culture will get it twisted every time. Without God at the center, it's hard to know whether things should be labeled as "good" or "evil." We must be serious students of Scripture to know the way God Himself sees events and issues. "Good" and "evil" isn't determined by the latest update from our favorite podcaster or the one news source that we consume. Our evaluations of good and evil should be based on His Truth rather than our opinions, talking heads, or experts in their field.

The Redeeming Work of Calling Out

When Esther confronted Haman, she couldn't calculate Haman's response or the king's. She had fasted and planned, but the whole thing could have caved in on her. If the king would have taken offense over having one of his main men accused or if he had felt that the accusation included himself, she could have been stepping out at her own peril. He had approved the edict she was contesting after all!

From reading the whole chapter, we know that Haman's doom was sealed the instant the sin was labeled, and the truth was spoken. There was no opportunity for Haman's redemption.

But often, calling out evil is used in Scripture to open the door for repentance, a redeeming work of God.

Read 2 Samuel 12:1–14. Why do you think Nathan told a story to illustrate a hard truth? To expose David's sin?

____

____

____

____

How does verse 5 tell us that David felt at the end of Nathan's story? What did he say that the punishment should be for the evil-doer?

How would you describe Nathan's follow-up words to David? Why do you think he led with the story and followed with this message directly from God?

What was David's response?

What were the gifts the Lord gave to David for his response? What was the consequence?

Nathan had the position of prophet. As such, he was a truth-teller, speaking the words of God directly. He understood that human response to truth wasn't his responsibility. Sometimes truth-telling leads to dire consequences, like Haman. But truth-telling can lead to repentance and lesser consequences, like David.

As a young woman, God began to bring a series of mentors, truth-telling women who loved me well, into my life. These women taught me about grace but also held my feet to the fire when needed. After the first mentor, my dear Layne who lived in the trailer in my parents' backyard for a year, I was addicted. I began to seek out my "Nathan" in every season of life. It's one of my values to surround myself with loving truth-tellers. I'm older now, and I'm stepping into that role for younger women coming along behind me. It's a truth-teller sandwich. I have truth-tellers, and I've become a truth-teller.

Who are the loving truth-tellers in your life? If you haven't currently invited someone in, who might you seek out in your current context or beyond (think aunts, cousins, former influential women in your life)?

How does reading the story of Nathan and David re-shape the idea of truth-telling presented between Esther and Haman?

Where do you see value in each approach?

How does the hearer's response play into the role of truth-telling?

What's lost in the life of Christ-followers if we erase the voices of truth-tellers like Esther and Nathan?

Jesus sets the standards for our truth-telling. Even while showing lavish love and grace, He drew firm lines for sinners against evil. In the story of the adulterous woman being stoned, we see both when He says, "'Then neither do I condemn you,' Jesus declared. 'Go now and leave your life of sin'" (John 8:11).

Jesus spoke harsher words of truth against the evils of self-righteousness to the religious. For example, He called the Pharisees and Sadducees a "brood of vipers" (Matthew 3:7).

Every word Jesus spoke came directly from His Father, so every word was imbued with all of who the Father is (John 8:28), including truth that confronted evil. He sets the standard for those who love Him.

Redemption, not revenge, is the ultimate goal when we call out evil.

When and where are Jesus-followers called to speak up against evil?

What happens when godly people don't speak up?

What happens when godly people speak up in the wrong ways?

One notorious historic example of the failure of the church to speak up against evil was during Adolf Hitler's reign of Nazi Germany in the World War II era. Dietrich Bonhoeffer, an anti-Nazi theologian and pastor who ultimately gave his life in opposition to Hitler, famously said, "Silence in the face of evil is itself evil: God will not hold us guiltless. Not to speak is to speak. Not to act is to act."[5]

As Jesus followers, there will be times when we're called to label evil with its correct label, speaking up against it, condemning actions or policies (edicts!) that hurt others even if we can hide from the effects ourselves. Just like Esther, we are called to vanquish evil and champion life.

Pathway Principle

Godly people call out evil for redemption, not revenge.

Memorize

Today, fill in the blanks. Then read the verse aloud into a recording device. Listen to it four times while you're reading it.

"She ________ with wisdom, and ______________instruction is on her ________" (Proverbs 31:26).

Application

When have you been in a situation where evil was being tolerated or even mistaken for good?

How would it help (have helped) to give evil an appropriate label?

In what area might God call you to speak up in an evil situation, potentially ushering in redemption?

Day Four: Speak Up with Perseverance

"I don't like this calling. I knew it was going to be terrible!"

In a low moment, following a week filled with harsh criticism coming my way, I spat these words out of my mouth. I was tired. I was discouraged. I was *done.*

Callings have seasons, and God gave my calling a big left turn several years ago. For about a decade, I talked to others about ending our own perfectionism so that God could begin His perfecting work in us. I wrote two books, *Breaking Up with Perfect* and *Exhale,* blogged and began to co-host Grit 'n' Grace the Podcast during that time, and all was well. I'm not saying there weren't bumps in the road, but it was pretty palatable stuff for most people. As a result, I got very little push back.

But God had new ideas for me. He began taking me on a personal journey to listen, feel, do, and speak, and then He called me to gather a community of women who are developing tender hearts and strong voices. It's the strong voice part people don't love so much, and I started to receive more criticism. I drew a hater or two. Because I'm not a girl who loves a good fight, the emotional toll of feeling embattled started to get to me.

I know giving up isn't an option, though. As hard as it is to walk in God's plans for us sometimes, it's even more painful to walk away.

Have you ever been there? Running from God? Ignoring His promptings? Blazing your own path? If you have, then you know hustling, wrestling, and disobeying are more awful than life with God could ever be.

Not. Worth. It.

If giving up isn't an option for you either, then we have to find ways to persevere, to hang on when speaking up gets tough. Esther is a good example for us because once she started speaking up, she kept at it, through both spoken and written words. She persevered and didn't stop short of achieving her life-saving goal.

Read Esther 7:6–8:2. How did the king respond to Esther's accusation against Haman?

How did Haman respond to Esther's accusation?

Describe the misunderstanding that ensued.

Who else spoke into the situation? What were *possible* motives for Harbona to speak up? (Note: I find this short speech by Harbona to be very interesting. Consistent with the rest of the book, there's no explanation of his motive.)

What was the end result?

Whew. In this dramatic scene we see another set of peripeties. These reversals are sudden and violent.

Fill in the blanks to show the reversals.

Haman boasts about his vast wealth and power (Esther 5:11) →

Haman builds a pole (some translations say "gallows") on which to impale or hang Mordecai (Esther 5:14) →

In God's providence, He uses both Esther and Harbona to bring about His justice and judgement upon Haman. While some commentators argue that Esther would have been a more honorable woman if she had spoken up for mercy for Haman, others state that Esther is simply fulfilling the divine plan that her ancestor Saul failed to complete.

For the rest of the book of Esther, we'll be faced with the tension of uncertainty, like with this scene of Esther watching silently while Haman is dragged away to be executed for allegedly assaulting her. We do so by both engaging our intellect and trusting our God.

Never, Never, Never Give Up

Read Esther 8:3–6. Why is Esther pleading with the king again? What's completed? What's still incomplete?

If Esther had gotten discouraged, let fear rise, and given up, what would have been the result?

What is an incomplete outcome in your life?

How might you need to persevere to see that outcome come to full fruition?

Once again, Esther is putting her life in peril. Once again, the king extends his scepter to her, and she reminds him of an important truth. Her enemy is dead, but her people are still slated for annihilation. Although she had already prepared two feasts and spoken up once, she had to hang in there until the task was complete. Esther persevered.

Perseverance is a key component of living a victorious Christian life. Other translations use the words "endurance" or "long-suffering" as a synonym, but the NIV version uses "perseverance" more often. Look up the verses below in an NIV translation (If you don't own one, you can find it at BibleGateway.com) to see how perseverance is developed.

Read each verse and write how perseverance is forged.

Romans 5:3–4

2 Thessalonians 1:4

James 1:3

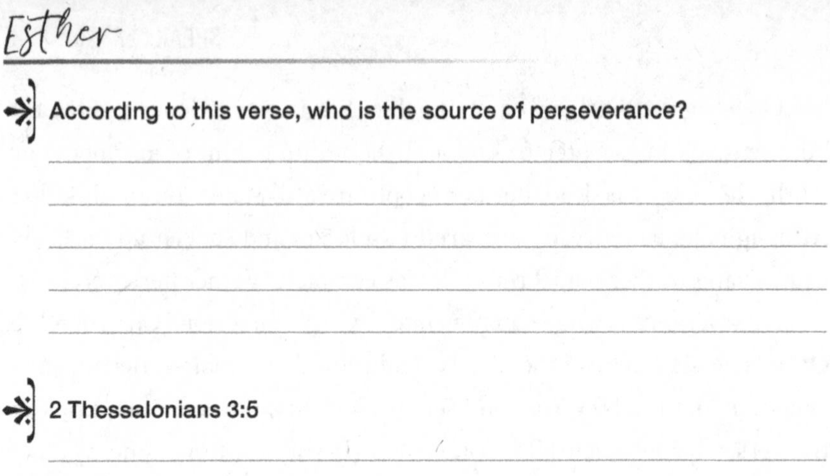

According to this verse, who is the source of perseverance?

2 Thessalonians 3:5

From your answers, you can probably see what's clear to me now, too. Esther came by her stick-to-itiveness the hard way. Her trials trained her. All those hard seasons of her life are coming in handy now. She has the chutzpah, extreme self-confidence or audacity, needed to bring her mission home.

Perseverance is a hard-won but crucial virtue to live your one life well. Thankfully, we don't have to refine our own character simply through suffering. We have a source of perseverance.

Embrace the Divine Partnership

In Psalm 81:10, God gives a promise of partnership to those who have steadfastly committed to be His mouthpiece. He says, "I am the Lord your God, who brought you up out of Egypt. Open wide your mouth and I will fill it." This passage is given in the context of God's provision in the desert for the Israelites as they came out of Egypt, but it's also a principle for those who are speaking up under the guidance of the Holy Spirit.

There are two parts to this promise. One is our part, and one is God's alone.

1. He commands us to "open wide your mouth." These are the steps of anticipatory obedience we take. Esther was a great example for us. We've watched her:
   a. Accept wise counsel from Mordecai.
   b. Enlist a community of her household staff.
   c. Fast for strength and favor.

When we're preparing to step into our unique usefulness, we can follow these same steps of obedience.

A. Accept wise counsel by learning from experts, reading books by trusted authors, taking classes, or attending conferences.
B. Enlist a community of friends or step into a vetted organization.
C. Fast for strength and favor.

I also love that we are to open "wide"! Not just a little. Not only a crack. We anticipate the goodness of the Lord's provision, and we open *wide* our mouths.

2. We prepare, and we pray for provision. As our friend Lysa TerKeurst says, "We do everything that we can do, and we pray for God to do what only He can do." He fills our mouths with words. Powerful words. Words straight from the heart of the One who commanded everything to be made with creative, transforming words.

Read Luke 21:10–15. What does Jesus promise to provide for His followers when they are speaking for Him?

Read Mark 13:11. Who is the source of those words?

Read Luke 12:11–12. How do you feel reading these words?

God never gives us an assignment and then leaves us alone to achieve it. Although His name isn't spoken in the book of Esther, we have clearly been able to trace His hand. It's true in our lives, too. He gives us a unique usefulness, a place in His great story. God trains us in our trials, developing perseverance in us. Then He gives us steps of obedience to take in preparation. When it's time to speak up, He gives us words over and over again until His purposes are accomplished.

Although I had a moment of angst and doubt that I shared with you at the beginning of the study today, God gave me a good night's sleep, and I woke up renewed and ready to go again. His faithfulness covers my failings and calls me back every time. I'm learning that speaking up when the Holy Spirit fills my mouth is ultimately a blessing every time. I worry less and less about the pushback.

Our good God redeems the school-of-hard-knocks with the reward of perseverance. He also improves the impact of our voice with His own, filling every gap and providing each word. Even when we're handling haters, catching criticism, and massaging misunderstandings, we can know that God is with us.

Pathway Principle

Godly people keep speaking up even when it gets hard.

Memorize

Today, fill in the blanks. Once you're finished, read it aloud once while clapping your hands in rhythm.

" She _______ with __________, and ________ ________ is on her __________" (Proverbs 31:26).

Now try to say it aloud without looking. Don't worry about mistakes. Just use it as an opportunity to see what your brain hasn't "caught" yet. Read the sections aloud that you had trouble with several more times.

Application

Circle the number that best reflects your perseverance level.

(No perseverance) (Strong perseverance)

1 2 3 4 5 6 7 8 9 10

What life circumstances has God used to grow your perseverance in the past?

How might that help you see your current circumstances in a more positive light?

Day Five: Speak Up for Community in Community

When I was asked to lead a discussion group about racial equity, I gave an instant "yes!" As you know by now, this issue has become my unique usefulness. (I hope yours is emerging, too.) I knew the group to be open-hearted. It was an exciting opportunity to grow the understanding of people who had literally signed up for it.

But as the meeting grew nearer, unease sprouted in my heart. There was no doubt about my eagerness to help, but as a leader, I also had some undeniable and serious voids. My longevity in the area of racial equity is limited, and I have never had racism aimed at me. My gaps were potential traps, places that could hurt both myself and my audience. I had the passion, but I needed a partner.

Have you ever been in a position to speak but needed a partner to help fill your gaps? How did God provide? (Perhaps you are still waiting for the partner to show up—keep asking, keep trusting.)

Read Esther 8:7–17. This passage is an echo from Esther 3:12–14 with a twist. What new reversal occurs in chapter 8?

Whom are the two people God put into a speak-up partnership?

What had Esther's part of the partnership been?

What part is Mordecai accomplishing in this passage?

As a woman, I find this chapter of Esther particularly inspiring. It reveals a powerful, platonic partnership between a man and a woman, acting together to save other image bearers. Both Esther and Mordecai had essential jobs in rescuing God's people. This too is an echo of a much-earlier event.

Read Genesis 1:27. God created both male and female in His own image, so He embodies the beautiful traits of both male and female.

Drawing from your knowledge of Scripture and our culture, what traits of God are typically attributed to females?

Drawing from your knowledge of Scripture and our culture, what traits of God are typically attributed to males?

Read Genesis 2:15–25. Take another look at verse 18, "The Lord God said, 'It is not good for the man to be alone. I will make a helper suitable for him.'" The original word that's translated "helper" is "ezer." This word is fascinating, because it's used twenty-one times total in the Bible.

In Genesis 2, "ezer" is used twice in regard to women. Subsequently, it's used sixteen more times in Scripture to describe God's strong help for Israel. It's a military term that describes God's fierce protection as Israel's "shield and defense." In light of the way the word is used throughout Scripture, Professor John McKinley says that a truer translation of "a helper fit for him" is a "necessary ally." "Necessary ally brings into view the joint mission for which the male and female are created to rule God's earthly kingdom."[6]

Esther and Mordecai are motivated to act *in community* with each other *for their community*. As our friend Dr. Joel Muddamalle said when we interviewed him before we started writing this study, "They're prompted to act, not out of the possibility of their own demise, but because of the demise of their people. There's a community ethic that's at play that cannot be missed. If we're too fast to be motivated by personal ambition or self-preservation, we may miss the opportune moment to act in the greater good of the people."

How does understanding the word "ezer" shift how you see Esther's relationship with Mordecai?

How does it strengthen your understanding of Esther's part in the historical event we're studying?

How does it clarify the necessity of both Esther and Mordecai in this divine rescue?

Speaking Up *to* Somebody

God's character is most fully displayed when His full image—both male and female—is employed.

We see this over and over again in Scripture. God uses a woman's voice alongside a man's to bring about His purposes. Let's take a look at a couple instances to see what we can learn.

Read 2 Kings 22:8–18. Who did the king's advisors "inquire of the LORD" from about the book found in the temple? (Extra credit: What was the book?)

How is she described?

The first words out of her mouth were, "This is what the Lord, the God of Israel, says . . ." What adjectives would you use to describe the way in which she spoke up?

How did the men treat her words?

Skim 1 Samuel 25. Who did God use to rescue her community from David's wrath?

How would you describe her? How would you describe her speech to David?

Uninvited, Esther approached her volatile husband with requests that would save her people. A group of male leaders came to Huldah, a woman who they clearly trusted, and asked for God's very words. Abigail took the initiative to deliver strong advice to an angry man in a winsome way.

Esther, Abigail, and Huldah lived up to the powerful title of *ezer.* They were necessary allies who came alongside men in their hard circumstances to speak tender but strong words. The men's responses in these stories encourage me, too! King Xerxes, King Josiah, and future-king David were receptive and respectful to women's words.

In the gender-war that sometimes erupts in faith communities, these are accounts that should strengthen us to stand for strong partnerships between men and women. Male and female working and speaking up together is mutually beneficial. Like Esther and Mordecai, the unique strengths of the two were dovetailed to accomplish Kingdom work.

Speaking Up *with* Somebody

Years ago, I said "yes" to what I was sure would be the worst divine assignment of my life. I became a member of my church's pastor search committee. We were tasked with finding the new person who would replace our beloved pastor of almost thirty years.

I didn't know what to expect when I stepped into that first meeting of our committee, a group of two women and four men. It turned out to be the most enriching experience of my church life. Every gift in the room was employed, and each voice was valued. We all treated each other with the utmost respect.

That year showed me the unique power of men and women joining their gifts and voices in partnership. It gave me a glimpse of what might be possible if all we Jesus-people, like Esther and Mordecai, stepped fully up to the plate to build God's Kingdom.

Words are powerful. How does knowing God gave the word *ezer* to describe both women and Himself empower you to use your voice for Him?

Who are some men in your circle who would affirm your voice and might be open to Kingdom partnerships in your unique usefulness? If you can't think of anyone, pray and ask God to show you a brother who encourages women's gifts or to bring such a man into your faith community.

A Girl Squad

Read Numbers 27:1–11. What were the names of Zelophehad's daughters? (These are doozies, right?!)

Why did they go to speak up to Moses, the high priest, and the whole assembly?

What might have been the advantages to going together?

As you consider what you know of these ancient times, what might the risks have been to going alone? What were the risks even in going as a group?

What was the outcome?

It's not only scriptural for women to partner with men in speaking up. As you see in this passage, women partner with other women effectively, too. Lynn's study, *Fearless Women of the Bible*, includes a deeper study of this scene, and her book was the first time I had ever delved into this obscure passage. It might be buried a bit, but it's rich.

By joining their voices together, these sisters spoke up for justice, preserving their family name and lands, and prevailed. Moses, one of the strongest leaders ever known, paid attention, heard their petition, and honored their boldness. They made sure that the land was passed down from generation to generation.

The Daughters of Z, as Lynn affectionately calls them, passed down the land, but other women have also made sure that justice, faith, and the stories of God's people are passed from one generation to the next. The word "tradent" is a word of Rabbinic or Jewish origin that means "a person who hands down or transmits (especially oral) tradition."[7] In other words, in Jewish tradition, a tradent is one who makes sure that the next generation hears God's story.

Esther was a tradent who made sure that the next generation lived to tell the story. There are other tradent sisters sprinkled through the whole story of Scripture. Here's one of my New Testament favorites.

Read Luke 2:21–40. (You can skim the beginning for time's sake, but slow down when you get to verse 36.) In verse 38, who speaks to "all who were looking forward to the redemption of Jerusalem"?

How can you see her fulfilling the role of a tradent?

There's another tradent present who is silent in this passage. Who is the most likely person to have told this account to Luke whose written account was then passed to generations of those who love Jesus?

I'm in awe as I think of young Mary and old Anna, both powerful tradents, standing in the temple together, wrapped in the glory of the Messiah. My sanctified imagination pictures Mary, who in the moment had silently marveled and treasured up all these things in her heart (Luke 2:19), when Luke asks her years later for all the details. Can you imagine the bittersweet joy of telling Doctor Luke, the historian, following Jesus' death and resurrection, all about Her precious sons' birth? I'm in tears thinking about Mary as the tradent who spoke up and passed the story of Jesus' birth and childhood to us.

When we're called to speak up in our unique usefulness, we're almost never alone. God kindly surrounds us with others to champion the same cause and to support us in friendship. The day I faced the reality of my own inability to lead our group in a conversation about racial equity, God brought to mind a new friend, a young woman of color, whom I knew could fill my gaps. I reached out to her, and she agreed to partner with me to lead the meeting. Each of us brought our gifts and our unique perspectives, creating an experience for the rest of the group that was far more powerful than I could have created by myself.

I'm immeasurably grateful to Esther, Huldah, Abigail, the Daughters of Z, Mary, and Anna for showing us what it's like to be ezers and tradents, speaking up in partnership with men and other women. But more than that, I'm thankful to God, our Creator, who includes the important stories of women in His Word. He is the One for whom we speak up in our unique usefulness.

Pathway Principle

God uses the collective voices of His people, both men and women, to protect and build His Kingdom.

Memorize

"She speaks with wisdom, and faithful instruction is on her tongue" (Proverbs 31:26).

Today, cover our memory verse with your hand and repeat it four times. Peek without shame if you need to!

Application

Find two notecards. On one write "I am an ezer." On the other write "I am a tradent." Put them somewhere you'll see them every day and ask God each day how to live out these truths about yourself.

Prayerfully collect a group of women who desire to live the same calling, to be both an ezer and a tradent. Spend time supporting each other in your unique usefulness.

Speak Pathway Principles

God uses women's voices in their unique usefulness to build His Kingdom from one generation to the next.

Godly people speak up in godly ways.
Godly people speak up for both spiritual and physical life.
Godly people call out evil for redemption, not revenge.
Godly people keep speaking up even when it's hard.
God uses the collective voices of His people, both men and women, to protect and build His Kingdom.

Prayer

Lord, You have created me with a unique usefulness. I choose to walk away from self-protective silence and to be a tradent instead. Like Esther, I want to use my voice for good in the world. It's a joy to be part of Your story and to use my voice to make sure Your truths continue to the next generation. In Jesus' name, Amen.

Questions for Discussion or Personal Journaling

1. Whom do you see as a role model of a godly person who speaks up in godly ways? Why do you see them as a role model?

2. Which of the Proverbs from day 1 did you personally need the most? Why?

3. How has God used your words in the past to give life to someone in a hard circumstance?

4. What is one new thing you learned directly from the Scripture reading this week?

5. Which of the ideas from this week resonated with you the most? How will you apply this idea in your life next week?

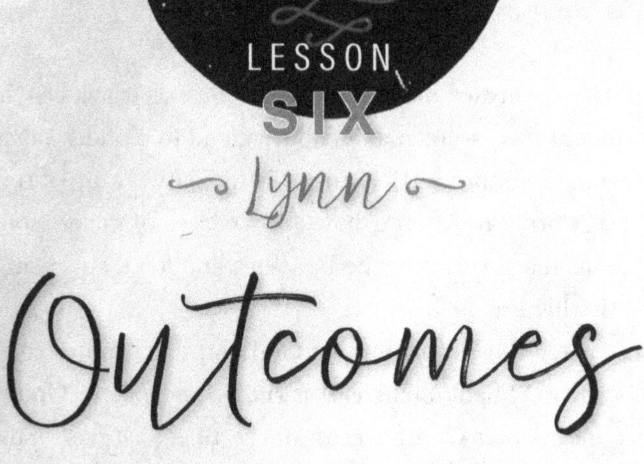

Day One: Impossible Outcomes

Hi! It's Lynn again . . . the gal whose husband got a job by her giving him her job. That's not the only time when I didn't see the outcome that was coming.

I had experienced this turning of events before with God. Remember the story of me and giving up my lifelong crush in week 4? Several months later, my time of training at the discipleship school came to an end. The next stop for me would be another one thousand miles away to go and help my sister and her husband as they planted a new church. In between moves, I would stop at home and spend a few weeks with my parents.

It's a bit awkward to move home once you've made the big jump out of your parent's nest, but after settling into my old bedroom once again, I also headed back to our home church. And who should be there? The boy-turned-man that I had crushed on for years. Long story short, we dated for six weeks, got married in ten months, and have now been married for over thirty-five years! Did you see that coming? I sure didn't!

So can be the way of God. Unpredictability is often the mark of uncertainty when we're walking with Him. We always have to be prepared for His reversals!

We ended last week with the decree sent out allowing "the Jews in every city the right to assemble and protect themselves; to destroy, kill and annihilate the armed men of any nationality or province who might attack them and their women and children, and to plunder the property of their enemies" (Esther 8:11). Esther 9 is the outworking of this decree and not just Mordecai's decree, but God's decree of generations before to bring about the survival of the Israelites and for their enemies to be destroyed (Esther 9:1–19).

We often see these workings of God and don't quite have a word to describe them. Theologians call it the providence of God. "Divine providence means that God governs all creatures, actions, and circumstances through the normal and ordinary course of human life, without the intervention of the supernatural."[1] In short, it means "God is for us".[2]

Let's get an overview for our week by reading Esther 9.

This chapter begins with what feels like a report ". . . the Jews got the upper hand over those who hated them" (Esther 9:1). "The outcome of the conflict had already been settled before it began because 'the tables were turned.'"[3]

Even though we don't hear His name, we see God's providence all throughout the book of Esther. We see Him over every action and every detail that takes place, all the while not using any miraculous means to do so. But He sure does use the plot twist!

Scholars call these twists of events, the theme of reversals. I've noted below the reversals I found by reading this chapter. Draw a line from each reference to the reversal listed.

Esther 9:1	The Jews struck their enemies.
Esther 9:2	Fear of the Jews fell on the people.
Esther 9:3	Haman and sons are hanged.
Esther 9:5	The Jews gained mastery over the Persians.
Esther 9:22	Sorrow turned to gladness, mourning into a holiday.
Esther 9:25	Officials, satraps and governor's help the Jews.

Reading Esther 9:1 in many different versions gives us the full view of God's work:

"... the reverse occurred" (ESV)
"but now the tables were turned" (NIV)
"but quite the opposite happened" (NLT)
"but their plan was overturned" (BSB)
"it was turned to the contrary" (KJV)
"the opposite occurred" (NKJV)
"it happened the other way around" (AMP)
"just the opposite happened" (CSB)

How does verse 3 describe how the Persians viewed Mordecai?

Again, we see a reversal. The powerful Persians had demanded "fear" or respect *from* Mordecai, but in the end, it was the Persians fearing Mordecai. What seemed impossible in chapters 3 and 4 has become a reality in the end.

Daily, there are situations in our lives, when we have no idea what our outcome will be. Yet, we can take hope from the story of Esther, that even when we cannot see the outcome, our God is at work, creating an ending that will glorify Himself. The outcome may not be what we wanted, expected, or planned, but as we set our intention to live as Jesus taught us to pray, "your kingdom come, your will be done, on earth as it is in heaven" (Matthew 6:10), we can trust that the outcome will be one that will glorify our King.

Pathway Principle

Even when we cannot see the outcome, our God is at work, creating an ending that glorifies Himself.

Memorize

"For nothing will be impossible with God" (Luke 1:37 ESV).

Read the memory verse aloud four times. Read it very slowly the first time and faster each subsequent time.

Application

Write out again the "impossible" you struggle to see God's hand in. Behind it write out today's verse. "For nothing will be impossible with God" (Luke 1:37). Take a moment to voice to Father that you believe He is at work, even when you cannot see His hand.

Day Two: Outcomes Even for Less than Perfect People

Exasperated and at the end of my rope, I was doing all I could to keep my cool. My teenage child just could not understand why my answer was no and simply would not let up until they did. Unwilling to continue a conversation I felt I couldn't win, I prepared to give *myself* a time out. On the verge of losing all self-control, I said I was done talking for now to which they replied, "Why when you are really mad, do you spit at me with clenched teeth?" Oh my!

This mom . . . Well, she simply was a very poor role model at that moment.

As I am studying chapter 9, I'm wondering if Queen Esther is also not a great role model for us at *this* particular moment in her story.

Review Esther 9:11–15 and write out the specific additional request Esther asked of the king after the first day of the Jews destroying their enemies.

____

____

____

____

It's possible Esther was following God's lead, as it appears she had been doing, in asking the king for the second day of destroying her enemies. She had fasted. Perhaps this second day, God was taking out additional enemies and using a king to destroy people who were trying to destroy the Jews. As God spoke in Deuteronomy 25:19, "Therefore, when the Lord your God has given you rest from all your enemies in the land he is giving you as a special possession, you must destroy the Amalekites and erase their memory from under heaven. Never forget this!" (NLT), His intentions now with those who hated His people could be the same. We have no record of God giving this direction at this time to Esther. (Just as we have not seen direct communication in the rest of the book.) The killing that was taking place in chapter 9, though, was not just those with a history connected to the Amalekites, but all people who hated the Jews (Esther 9:1).

But, maybe, I've been wondering, Esther believed "we deserve this." We deserve to take revenge on those who hate us and so she asked for what she believed the Jews should have: a second day of killing.

Just this morning, I was reading in my Bible of David, the future king of Israel. Over and over the Bible tells us David asked the Lord for direction before he made a move (1 Samuel 30:8; 2 Samuel 5:19–20, 23–25). This man, who God Himself says was a man after His own heart, repeatedly sought God for each step he took; until he didn't (1 Chronicles 15:13). Somewhere along the way, between a shepherd boy brave enough to face a giant and king leading the entire nation of Israel, David's heart began slipping away from the Lord. One fateful afternoon, he chose to be a man after the desires of *his* own heart, a man who wanted more than anything else to fulfill those desires. One step of sleeping with a woman married to someone else led to a slippery slope ending in adultery and eventually murder (2 Samuel 11–12).

Often in our reflecting on the man David, we focus on Goliath and the bravery of a boy who trusted God to see him through. It's good to see David in this light, but it is also important for us to see that this same man of God failed, for this part of David's story tells another important side of God.

God uses even people who fail.

The day God called Samuel to anoint David, God knew David would fall one day, and yet He still chose him.

Maybe, as David grew up, and his positions changed from shepherd to harpist to commander of Israel's army and eventually king, the way he saw himself changed as well. Maybe on that fateful afternoon, as he was captured by the beautiful Bathsheba bathing, he began to let himself believe "I deserve her." And he listened to the voice of pride, the same voice that speaks to us all.

What might have been Esther's motivation for the *second* day of killing she requested of the king in Esther 9:13?

David and Esther, while both used by God in extraordinary ways, were also humans prone to temptation just as we are.

Even when we are fulfilling the assignments God has given us, we can allow our emotions and feelings to kick in, causing us to not act as our Master. Yes, He is a God of justice, but could it be that by requesting a second day Esther was taking things into her own hands?

The Bible doesn't let us in on her thoughts as ". . . Esther said, "'If it pleases the king,' Esther answered, 'give the Jews in Susa permission to carry out this day's edict tomorrow also, and let Haman's ten sons be impaled on poles'" (Esther 9:13). No, we don't know her thoughts, but it would appear that this isn't a side of the queen we should copy.

As I pondered this possible side of the queen, I consulted commentaries to see how they viewed this second day. In *The NIV Application Commentary*, Karen Jobes writes, "Both Christian and Jewish interpreters have found Esther's request morally troubling . . . for this horrible request no justification can be found."[4] C. A. Moore observes Esther as a "deceitful and bloodthirsty woman . . . but unless one is willing to judge Esther's outward act in complete isolation, without any real knowledge of the external circumstances, then one's judgment must be tentatively made."[5] Jobes writes, "Michael Fox points out that given the stipulations of Haman's decree, the Jews' enemies could not lawfully have attacked them on a second day. Therefore, the Jews were safe, and Esther's request was literally overkill."[6] "The biblical Esther is evaluated almost universally in negative terms for requesting a second day of killing."[7]

If this was in fact what took place, Esther isn't the only one who struggled with giving in to corrupt feelings reeling inside. "The Bible is remarkable in revealing the darker side of God's chosen leaders, often just at their shining moment."[8]

I think many of us can remember a time when we experienced that rush—an ungodly, ugly happiness—when someone "got what they deserved". It's a full blown, in-the-flesh moment when our old self delights in someone else's payback. Especially when we are in times of uncertainty, sometimes it can feel good when someone else has it worse than we do.

Let's call it what it is, sin. Esther may have been experiencing this when she asked the king to add another day of destruction to his decree.

Maybe the power Esther was now experiencing was beginning to go to her head. Pride slithering into her heart. Commentary writer Karen Jobes suggests: "Perhaps he [the author] is suggesting that no one, Jew or Gentile, can handle power without yielding to its dark side. Perhaps Esther's request for a second day of killing shows that she herself had begun to feel the heady intoxication of the power she had so remarkably attained. Even as others in the court have manipulated Xerxes for their own agendas, Esther also has now learned to exercise her power over Xerxes for her own purposes."[9] Had Xerxes' reckless abuse of power which Esther witnessed over and over again, rubbed off on her?

When have you experienced the intoxication of influence? Think of all the different roles you hold in life: mother, wife, daughter, employer, ministry leader, volunteer coordinator, committee lead, etc.

Few people have the ability to put off the allurement power offers us. Our old nature relishes attention, approval, and authority over others. Power brings about a glory of sorts and not one of us was created for this glory. We were not made to be elevated. We simply cannot handle the glory that is only God's to carry. Think of God's chief enemy, Satan. He was permanently cast out of God's plan and purpose for creation because of his pride; because he wanted to carry the glory of God himself (Isaiah 14:12–16; Ezekiel 28:13–19).

Esther was a specific woman fulfilling a specific assignment from God during a specific period of time. She was a woman who demonstrated bravery and courage, but certainly not a woman without faults. For this reason, as those who follow Christ, we can study her story and learn many great truths, but let's be careful to not lift her up as the *perfect* role model to emulate for our lives today.

Looking at Esther's shortcomings does not strip away the lessons we have been learning from her. In fact, facing this side of Esther can do just the opposite.

No past mistakes, present poor decisions, or future sins disqualifies you and me from being used by God, if we will choose to humble ourselves, ask for forgiveness, turn from following our own path against God, and choose to draw close to Him again.

James 4:8 gives us both this promise and this command: "Come near to God and he will come near to you. Wash your hands, you sinners, and purify your hearts, you double-minded." God may actually use our own shortcomings to give glory to Himself. That He can and does use someone for His purposes just like us is astounding.

Perhaps you have already experienced God using your past errors to show off His greatness. If so, give Him thanks and praise in the space below.

____

____

____

____

____

Pathway Principle

We can learn from biblical characters, but it is the Lord we emulate.

Memorize

"For nothing will be impossible with God" (Luke 1:37 ESV).

Today, write out the memory verse 4 times and then read all four times aloud. Circle words that are meaningful to you.

Application

Looking back on your past errors, where specifically might God use you and those exact mistakes to help others learn His ways?

Are you ready for this to begin?

Day Three: It's Not Yours to Take (or Obedience and Outcomes)

After the completion of a tough job or a hard-won goal, nothing feels quite like praise. The "atta-girl" or "way-to-go" when you've finally reached the end of a long road can make all the tough work feel worthwhile.

And isn't there a part of us that feels like it's our right to soak in the "well done" when we worked so hard?

These feelings of "it's my right" are not new with you and me; they've probably been around as long as the first family. Maybe Eve felt it was her right to eat the fruit (Genesis 3). Cain may have felt he had the right to God's approval after bringing the offering of the fruit of the ground (Genesis 4:1–16). What we know for sure was each of them took something that wasn't theirs to take—Eve the fruit and Cain the life of his brother.

Read Esther 9:10, 15, 16. What important phrase occurs in these verses?

Plunder isn't a common word we use today. It means:

1. To take the goods by force, or without right; to pillage; to spoil; to sack; to strip; to rob; as, to plunder travelers.
2. To take by pillage; to appropriate forcibly; as, the enemy plundered all the goods they found.[10]

Why do you think the Jews did not lay hands on the plunder? Was it due to a law of King Xerxes' they were obeying? Was it a requirement from God as they fought for their lives?

Let's dig some more to see if we can uncover the answer to this question.

In Esther 8:11, what does Mordecai write in the name of King Xerxes concerning the plunder?

"Mordecai's decree included the permission to plunder because he was reversing the exact terms that Haman's decree had previously established."[11] Yet, even though Mordecai allowed the Jews to "plunder their goods", the Jewish people did not take a thing.

I wonder if this was because they had learned from their past.

I have seen in my own life: Looking back helps prevent mistakes as I move forward. The Jewish people had hundreds of years of history to look back on and learn from.

In the Old Testament, when God sent His people to perform holy war in His name, His instructions were for complete destruction. The people were not to keep any goods from the enemy or profit personally from plundering. When they obeyed God in this rule, they saw His blessing, as seen in the story of the fall of Jericho (Joshua 6:20–24) .When they did not obey God and chose to take what was not theirs to take, they suffered and experienced their own devastation as in the defeat at Ai (Joshua 7:11–12).

Look up and read Joshua 7:11–12 and 1 Samuel 15:18–19. If the Jews in Esther's day looked back at the mistakes their ancestors made under the leadership of Joshua, and the kingship of Saul, what might they have learned and applied here in Esther 9?

Can you think of a time in your life when you have done something your way instead of God's way and as a result, you did not experience the outcome you wanted or hoped for? Write it down. It's easier to learn when we acknowledge it.

Later, in 1 Samuel 15:20–21, Saul argues with Samuel that he kept some of the goods in order to make a sacrifice to God, the slaughtering of an animal for the forgiveness of sins or as an act of worship.

What are Samuel's famous words in 1 Samuel 15:22–23?

God wants the worship of obedience instead of the worship of sacrifice.

Back in 1 Samuel 15, when God had told Saul to completely take out the ancestors of Haman, the Amalakites, Saul did not obey. He kept some of the good stuff for himself. The Jews of Esther obeyed God's previous commands of not keeping any of the plunder. By not repeating the sin of Saul, the Jews finally had complete victory.

As we wrap up our study of the book of Esther and look at outcomes and obedience, the Bible has much to say.

Read Psalm 40:8. How does David describe his emotions with regard to living his life God's way?

David's delight to obey God gives God great delight as well!

I remember hearing an old saying when I was growing up, "It's easier to ask for forgiveness than to ask for permission."

Read Proverbs 21:3. What do you think God thinks of this type of thinking based on this verse?

As we see, obedience is important to God. In the Old Testament, the people of God were required to bring an animal sacrifice for the forgiveness of their disobedience. God made it very clear: He preferred obedience to all of their sacrifices.

Obedience is better than any offering we can give.

Look up the following passages below and write out the obedience God requires of those who follow Him.

Micah 6:6–8

Mark 12:28–34

Bible Nerd Box

For more on outcomes and obedience, see Matthew 8:13; Isaiah 1:11–20; Jeremiah 7:22–23; and Hosea 6:6.

Just as the Jews of Esther learned from the mistakes and sins of their ancestors, you and I can do the same. Without passing judgment, we can observe the wrong turns those around us have taken and choose to obey God the first time. Thankfully, when we miss and sin, we have the promise of forgiveness from our Savior, who was the perfect and final sacrifice.

Pathway Principle

Obedience is our part; outcomes are God's.

Memorize

Today, fill in the blanks. Once you're finished, read it aloud once while clapping your hands in rhythm.

"For ____________ will be __________ with God" (Luke 1:37 ESV).

Application

Moving forward, what does obedience look like for you? (There is no pressure here or hidden agenda for you to do anything other than listen to the Holy Spirit and follow.)

Remember: "The LORD makes firm the steps of the one who delights in him" (Proverbs 37:23).

Day Four: The Outcome Is a Celebration

I looked Greg directly in the eyes and simply stated, "I'm sad." My heart had been heavy all week and was tired of trying to be positive. For the second Easter in a row, we would not attend church in person because of COVID-19. Although I had read through the passion of Christ in the gospels that week, I wanted more. I wanted to celebrate with my brothers and sisters in Christ all He has done for us, and I wanted to do it in person.

The Old Testament tells us that our God is a God of celebration and memorializing. Throughout the Pentateuch, the first five books of the Bible, God calls His people to observe various festivals as a means of remembering what He has done as well as for teaching future generations to know His works as well.

Bible Nerd Box

For your own study of the seven main festivals or feasts of the Lord, look to Leviticus 23; Numbers 28–29; and Deuteronomy 16.

As we read in Esther 9:17–18, the initial day of feasting and gladness appears to be a natural outpouring of celebrating God's grand reversal. "This happened on the thirteenth day of the month of Adar, and on the fourteenth they rested and made it a day of feasting and joy. The Jews in Susa, however, had assembled on the thirteenth and fourteenth, and then on the fifteenth they rested and made it a day of feasting and joy."

Little did the people know they were creating a holiday that is still being observed by Jews today.

It didn't take long for Mordecai to record all the glorious details of God's plot twist and send this documentation to all of the Jewish people, calling on them to make this celebration an annual event.

Read Esther 9:17–32. Here the details of a new festival for the Jewish people are inaugurated. As you read these details, circle which ones applied to this first celebration.

1. Feasting and gladness
2. Sacrifices to God
3. Fasting
4. Remembering what God had done
5. Sending gifts of food to one another
6. Burning an effigy of Haman on a gallows

The name for this celebration would become *Purim*. This word, *Purim*, only occurs here in the book of Esther and was integrated into the Hebrew language, adding *-im* to the word *pur*.[12]

What does the word *pur* mean: ____________ ____________. (See Esther 9:24)

Let's go back to Esther 3:7 where we see this root word for the first time.

Reread Esther 3:7. Why did Haman "cast lots"?

____

____

____

As we mentioned in week 2, casting lots is a "traditional way of seeking divine guidance or . . . for finding the most opportune time to do something."[13] This festival was named *Purim* after the lottery Haman made to find the date for annihilating the Jews.

While Haman used this casting the lot for direction from his gods, the Hebrews also used this method various times in the Old Testament for gaining direction from God.[14] In 1 Chronicles 24:31, casting lots was used to determine the duties of the high priest. This method was also used in the New Testament in Luke 1:9 when Zacharias is selected to burn incense and in Acts 1:24–26 for the selection of Matthias as a new member added to the eleven disciples after Judas' death.

There are other meanings for the word *lot* used in the Bible. It can mean a portion or an inheritance (Joshua 15:1; Psalms 125:3), as well as a destiny, as assigned by God (Daniel 12:13).[15] Maybe you've heard the saying it's her "lot in life," meaning someone's general situation in life.[16] Unfortunately, we often use this phrase when a person's situation is not very good. That's not the way the Bible uses the word "lot".

Read Psalm 16:5. Can you see how both the meaning *lot* as in *destiny* and *casting lots* both play out in the story of Esther? Describe the possible intersections of meanings in the space below.

Purim Today

Purim is still celebrated annually on the fourteenth day of the month of Adar in the Jewish calendar. It is considered the most fun-filled, action-packed day of the Jewish year.

Today, Jews celebrate the day of Purim with four special mitzvahs, one of the Torah's 613 Divine commands created for the forming of a bond between God who commands and man who performs.

Bible Nerd Box

Today Jews around the world celebrate Purim on one day, Adar 14, except those living in one of the cities traditionally considered walled at the time of Joshua, which include Jerusalem, Hebron, and Jericho, where Purim is celebrated on Adar 15.[17]

The first mitzvah is hearing the Megillah, the scroll telling the story of Esther. There are two readings: one on Purim night and one on Purim day. The Megillah, using an age-old tune, is read by a Megillah reader from a handwritten parchment scroll. When Haman's name is mentioned, noisemakers called *graggers* are twirled, or there is the stamping of feet also, to eradicate Haman's evil name.

The second is giving to the needy. Haman tried to wipe out all the Jewish people. Since they were unfortunate in this danger together, now they all celebrate together as well as care for others who are unfortunate. Jewish people are encouraged to give money or food to at least two needy people during the day of Purim. Synagogues also may collect money and participants are encouraged to give at least two coins. Anyone who asks for a donation receives a donation; the recipient's need is not verified in order to receive the gift.

The third means of celebration is giving gifts of food to friends. The tradition is to send a package containing at least two different ready-to-eat food items and/or beverages to at least one Jewish acquaintance during the daytime of Purim. Men send to men and women send to women. These gifts are not delivered in person, but by a third party, often children.

The fourth is feasting. Jews gather with family and possibly friends to celebrate this special meal. Traditionally, it begins before sundown and lasts well into the evening. The setting is made beautiful with tablecloths and candles and includes meat, wine, Jewish songs, and words from the Torah all with a celebratory spirit. There is singing, drinking, and laughter.

Esther 9:19 describes how the holiday is to be celebrated. Read it and note these ways below.

What resemblance do you see between this description and modern celebrations today?

On Purim, Jewish children, and some adults as well, dress in costumes with masks as a reflection of God's unseen hand in their rescue and how His hand was disguised by the events surrounding it. Children masquerade as a character that is good and cheerful such as Mordecai or Esther. Some synagogues, before the reading, will have a party which includes prizes for children.[18]

What was the outcome of Mordecai's writings in Esther 9:27–28?

Mordecai's words caused people to come together, to gather and celebrate and be encouraged and reminded: God is a promise keeping God.

Drawing people to come together for the purpose of remembering God and being renewed in our faith in Him is powerful. Remember, before this time period, these Jewish people had not returned to the Promised Land even though they had the opportunity to. For whatever reason, whether they had grown very comfortable in a land that was not their true home or because they found the obstacles to going "home" too great, they were the ones who were still in a place they didn't belong. Maybe one of God's purposes for allowing all that was awful in Haman's schemes was drawing His people to come together and remember Him.

From the beginning, our God has been a God of festivals, celebrations, and traditions to draw us to Himself and remember His good work and love in our lives.

This is why my heart was so missing celebrating Easter with others.

As a child raised in a Catholic home, I remember attending mass on Ash Wednesday, the Wednesday forty-six days before Easter Sunday marking the beginning of Lent. It is a day of repentance, fasting, reflection and ultimately celebration.[19] (Although as a child I didn't realize all it represented.) Maudy Thursday reflects on our Savior's last supper and new commandment to love one another as He had loved us. We attended Mass on Good Friday with various pieces of worship including communion and of course worshipped in church on Easter Sunday.

As a teen, the church my family was attending performed a play of the Passion of Christ each year at Easter. The powerful visual reminded us of all He has done for us.

Although we were isolated from others that COVID Easter weekend, Greg and I partook of communion with our children. We watched a movie on Jesus' final days and celebrated His resurrection and the new life we now have.

Which of your church's traditions are the most meaningful to you? How do you personalize them today? If you don't practice any traditions, which have you observed in other families you find interesting or drawn to trying some day?

You and I may not celebrate Purim today.

We *can* celebrate what God has reversed in our lives.

We were destined to live eternally separated from God because of our sin, yet because of Jesus, we can experience the best reversal of all. We have been spared and given eternal life. As Jesus spoke to Martha outside Lazarus' tomb: "I am the resurrection and the life. The one who believes in me will live, even though they die" (John 11:25).

Yes, let us celebrate often the outcome of His death for us: new life in Jesus!

Pathway Principle

We celebrate the outcomes God brings to us His children.

Memorize

Today, fill in the blanks. Once you're finished, read it aloud once while clapping your hands in rhythm.

"For __________ will be _____________ with __________." (Luke 1:37 ESV).

Now try to say it aloud without looking. Don't worry about mistakes. Just use it as an opportunity to see what your brain hasn't "caught" yet. Read the sections aloud that you had trouble with several more times.

How do you personally or with others celebrate what Christ has done for you? Is there an old tradition you would like to renew or a new tradition you would like to begin?

Day Five: Outcomes Lie in the Lord's Hands

Our pastor had just shared that our church was in need of a pickup truck for hauling materials as we built a new sanctuary. I listened to what he said but didn't really think anything of it. Yes, Greg and I had a pickup. Since the truck was my mode of transportation to work, the request certainly could not be made of us, I reasoned.

Shortly after the service, Greg dropped the bombshell "I think we're supposed to donate our truck." *That makes no sense* is all I could think. How could two people, one working in an office park and the other driving out of town in sales each day, function with one car? Greg assured me we would be fine, and it was what he felt we were to do. With a large question mark hanging over my head, I agreed, wondering how we would make it work.

A few weeks after giving away the truck, Greg and I pulled into the church parking lot, spotting the truck across the way. Covered in dust, with dents in its sides, our sad eyes connected. I'll honestly admit, there was some anger too. *Didn't they appreciate the sacrifice we made? Were still making? Did they not feel the need to take care of it because it was given to them?*

Sitting through the service, I wrestled with anger. It was then I felt the conviction of the Holy Spirit. *Did you two give the truck to Me, Lynn?* Yes, we had given the truck to the Lord. *Then you have done your part of obedience. The rest is up to me.* I can't say my emotions immediately fell into line, but I did begin to see where our part ended, and God's began.

It has been many years since Greg and I gave away our truck, but the lesson has been one we've reviewed often.

Our part is obedience.
God's part is the outcome.

Let's finish our study reading the only three verses that make up Esther 10. Why was Mordecai popular with his Israelite brothers?

___

___

___

___

Once again, we see a divine reversal. While Haman's purpose was for their destruction, Mordecai's position was for peace.

This verse subtly points us to examine our work and motivations again. *For whose welfare am I working?* Sometimes when I feel dissatisfied with the outcome of my work, it's an indication I need to ask myself: Is my work an outcome of my abiding in Christ or an outcome of my hustle, an attempt to bear fruit on my own?

My own pushing, hustling, and striving produces something, but I'm not so sure it's fruit, for Jesus says, "apart from me you can do nothing" (John 15:5).

God's desired outcome in our lives
is glory to *His* name.

God desires that our lives give Him praise, honor, and show off His splendor. "This is to my Father's glory, that you bear much fruit, showing yourselves to be my disciples" (John 15:8).

It's time for us to check our hearts. Check our motivation.

You and I were never made for glory.

We were made to give *God* glory.

Giving all the glory to God and none of the glory to me is not as difficult when I refuse to find my identity in my actions, but instead, my identity as His child is put into action.

Again, it's a full circle.

We are not looking for approval, acceptance, attention, or even love because we have already received what we need from our Savior.

Instead, because we are loved and we are His children, we are able to love others and serve them with no conditions attached to that love. As Jesus said, "My command is this: Love each other as I have loved you" (John 15:12).

As we do the work of Jesus on the earth today, there will be times when we will be discouraged, not unlike the Jews when they heard the decree of King Xerxes. Our culture today has trouble upon trouble. Even with so much trouble, Jesus calls you and me to keep doing His work on the earth until He comes. This can begin as we listen, feel, do, and speak.

Whether or not we see the change we are working for or sense that our work is making a difference, we can know that the pain and suffering we continually see in our communities and on our planet will not go on forever.

God, the savior of not just the Jewish people, but all people, will one day wipe out every Haman and every harm that our enemy, Satan, uses against us. Revelation 1:17–18 promises us, "When I saw him, I fell at his feet as though dead. Then he placed his right hand on me and said: "Do not be afraid. I am the First and the Last. I am the Living One; I was dead, and now look, I am alive for ever and ever! And I hold the keys of death and Hades," He "will wipe every tear from their eyes. There will be no more death or mourning or crying or pain, for the old order of things has passed away" (Revelation 21:4). He will make all things new (Revelation 21:5)![20]

And so, our entire book ends with these words: "Mordecai the Jew was second in rank to King Xerxes, preeminent among the Jews, and held in high esteem by his many fellow Jews, because he worked for the good of his people and spoke up for the welfare of all the Jews" (Esther 10:3).

While popularity is not the goal, Mordecai's actions are. That I, too, would be motivated and moved to seek the welfare of my people, which is all people because we are all God's creations created in His very image.

As we've seen in this story of God in the book of Esther, nothing is too far from His reach, and nothing is outside His ability to change. As the angel Gabriel said to a virgin who would bear the savior, "For nothing will be impossible with God" (Luke 1:37 ESV).

Read Luke 1:26–38. Can you see it? The Bible is filled with strength of women empowered by God, women like Mary and women like Esther.

You and I come from a strong line of strong women. And while many of these fearless women could not see what the future held, they trusted in the God they could hope in.

As we wrap up our study, I think we can admit that at times, there were tough and uncertain patches in Esther's story. In these places, we may have made some judgments about her, had some questions about her. Now, we can zoom out and see the whole picture of her story. And as we look at her whole story, may it give us comfort and hope in our *own* story. As incomplete and uncertain as it may be, God *is* at work. He is available to us even when we can't see Him present or sense His presence.

Yet, even when we don't see or sense Him, we can know, that like Esther, we are women of God. We can partner with God and believe, as the angel said, "For nothing will be impossible with God" (Luke 1:37 ESV).

Nothing.

Not a reversal of Jews triumphing over their enemies.
Not a job opening where there was no opening.
Not a wayward child coming to the Savior.
Not a husband returning to his family.
Not an addict being set free.
Not an anxious daughter finding peace.

Not a neighbor being healed.
Nothing will be impossible with God.

Pathway Principle

No outcome is impossible with God.

Memorize

"For nothing will be impossible with God" (Luke 1:37 ESV).

Today, cover our memory verse with your hand and repeat it four times. It's ok if you have to peek if you need to!

Application

Write out a prayer below, sharing with Father that you believe: "For nothing will be impossible with God" (Luke 1:37 ESV). Reflect on how often we saw Him do the impossible in the book of Esther and how He can do the impossible in your life as well.

Outcomes Pathway Principles

Even when we cannot see the outcome, our God is at work,
creating an ending that glorifies Himself.
We can learn from biblical characters, but it is the Lord we emulate.
Obedience is our part; outcomes are God's.
We celebrate the outcomes God brings to us His children.
No outcome is impossible with God.

Prayer

Father, obedience is rarely easy. Empower me to keep in the forefront of my mind the outcomes I want to see and the story I want to write, so that I choose obedience each and every time. In Jesus' name, Amen.

Questions for Discussion or Personal Journaling

1. Describe a time in your life when an outcome took place that you didn't see coming.

2. Is there a situation in your life where God currently feels "invisible"? How has this study impacted your faith to believe Him for the "impossible" in that situation?

3. In what ways has your perspective of Esther as a woman of God changed or been impacted as a result of your study?

4. From the beginning of the study to the end, are there ways that you see the process of doing good works for God differently?

5. Maybe you have heard the saying: "It's easier to ask for forgiveness than to ask for permission." What do you think God thinks of this type of thinking based on Proverbs 21:3?

6. Read Revelation 1:17–18 and Revelation 21:5. Describe the hope these verses give you.

Bible Study Tools Quick Reference

Tool #1: The Clarity Principle (Week One, Day One)

When we run across a difficult-to-understand passage of Scripture, don't rush to interpret it through our human lens or build a wonky theology, a belief system about God, around it. Instead, dig into the whole of Scripture, interpreting the unclear passages with the clear ones.

Tool #2: Identifying Genres (Week One, Day Two)

Discover the genre of each book in the Bible you study. Take the genre into consideration as you are studying it. Knowing it helps us to understand and interpret Scripture. The seven genres of the Bible are:

1. **Narrative**

   Narrative tells us what happened in a book or story, according to the author. Narrative includes books of the Bible or sections telling the story within a book, such as Exodus in the Old Testament. It tells the story of what happened as the Israelites left Egypt. There may be lessons woven into the story or the story may be simply for the purpose of transferring information.

2. **Poetry**

Psalms and sections of other books are written as poetry. Poetry uses expressive, emotive, and picture-creating words for communication.

3. **Wisdom**

The wisdom genre uses wise sayings to create pictures and patterns for how we are to build our lives. Proverbs, Job, and Ecclesiastes are examples of wisdom.

4. **Prophecy**

There are four major prophets in the Old Testament—Isaiah, Jeremiah, Ezekiel, and Daniel—as well as twelve minor prophets, which include the books of Hosea through Malachi. These books contain God's words to the Israelites. They contain warnings received from God and written down by the author to be passed down to the people, cautioning them and bolstering them during periods of pronounced spiritual and national danger. Mel Lawrenz writes, "We gain spiritual lessons from them about the disposition of God (e.g., disappointed, indignant, sorrowful, tender, caring), and the condition of the people addressed (e.g., frightened, disobedient, humbled, arrogant). We must read Old Testament prophetic books as God's challenge to the original audiences, and then we apply the lessons to our day."

5. **Gospels**

The first four books of the New Testament make up the Gospels: Matthew, Mark, Luke, and John. While they include narrative, they are more than simply the story of Jesus and His disciples, as they provide the basis for our faith in Jesus.

6. **Epistles**

   Written mostly by the apostle Paul, the epistles are letters in the New Testament which were written to either churches or individuals to provide us truth today.

7. **Apocalypse**

   Revelation and parts of the book of Daniel make up the apocalyptic genre in the Bible. Similar to prophecy, they also carry warnings but include a greater depth of symbolic language for studying a time yet to come.

Tool #3: Determining the Difference between Descriptive and Prescriptive (Week One, Day Two)

There are two main types of Scripture: *descriptive* and *prescriptive.* It's important to know the difference, because prescriptive Scripture contains directives from God. If we confuse descriptive and prescriptive Scripture, it can lead to interpretive trouble. A question to help tell the difference between the two types is to ask: Is the passage *describing* something (it happened) or is it *prescribing* something (it should happen)?

Tool #4: Using Commentaries (Week Two, Day Four)

Commentaries, utilized through books or apps, offer us many benefits. Kevin R. O'Brien wrote an article titled "5 Benefits for Using Bible Commentaries in Your Bible Study." A few of these benefits help:

1. **Cut through cultural barriers.**

   You and I don't live in Biblical times. Commentaries help us spot when our own assumptions are hindering our interpretation of God's Word.

2. **See behind the English.**

   Commentaries help us to understand God's Word originally written in languages that are probably not our first language, along with the differences in the time periods when they were written.

3. **Discover how the Bible is interconnected.**

   The Bible is one book with many pieces. Commentaries can help us discover how the different pieces are woven together and give us a more complete picture of the Bible as a whole.

Tool #5: Asking Questions (Week Two, Day Four)

If you Google the question "What questions should I ask when I study the Bible?", you'll get a variety of answers. I encourage you to do so!

I (Lynn) ask these three questions of almost every passage I read:

- What does this passage teach me about Jesus?
- What does this passage teach me about people?
- How does this passage challenge me to live in light of what I have read and learned?

Tool #6: Using Repeated Readings of One Passage (Week Three, Day Two)

Read through the passage the first time simply for content and understanding of the context. Read the same passage at least five times over the next five days. Read slowly and ask the Holy Spirit to show you more truths each time. Journal the riches God shows you.

Endnotes

Week One

1. Karen H. Jobes, *Esther: The NIV Application Commentary* (Grand Rapids, MI: Zondervan, 1999), 21.
2. Jobes, 31.
3. Gotquestions.org, https://www.gotquestions.org/descriptive-vs-prescriptive.html.
4. Matthew Henry, *Matthew Henry's Commentary on the Whole Bible: Complete and Unabridged in One Volume* (pp. 643–644). Peabody: Hendrickson.
5. Jobes, 94.
6. Jobes, 95.
7. Jobes, 108.
8. Jerry Sittser, *A Grace Disguised*, Zondervan, Grand Rapids, MI, 1995, p. 179.

Week Two

1. Debra Reid, *Esther (Tyndale Old Testament Commentaries)* (Downer's Grove, IL: InterVarsity Press, 2008), 75.
2. Bryan Stevenson, *Just Mercy: A Story of Justice and Redemption* (New York City, NY: Random House Publishing Group, 2015), 14.
3. https://www.webmd.com/mental-health/narcissism-symptoms-signs.
4. https://www.historycentral.com/dates/Babylonia/Women.html.
5. https://www.britannica.com/topic/eunuch.
6. Jobes, 111.
7. Beth McCord, *Enneagram Type 3* (Nashville, TN: Thomas Nelson, 2019), 2–6.

8. Barb Roose, *Surrendered: Letting Go and Living Like Jesus* (Nashville, TN: Abingdon Press, 2020), 110.
9. Adam S. McHugh, *The Listening Life* (Downer's Grove, IL: InterVarsity Press, 2015), 138.
10. Dietrich Bonhoeffer, *Life Together* (New York: Harper One, 2009), 97.
11. McHugh, 142.
12. Jobes, 116–118.
13. htttps://www.oxfordlearnersdictionaries.com/us/definition/english/echo-chamber.
14. Jobes, 119.
15. http://www.ancientgreece.co.uk/war/home_set.html.

Week Three

1. Philip Yancey, *Where Is God When It Hurts* (Grand Rapids, MI: Zondervan,1990), 231.
2. Matthew Henry, *Matthew Henry's Commentary on the Whole Bible* (Peabody, MA: Hendrickson Publishers, 1994), 646.
3. Jobes, 132.
4. Jobes, 134.
5. Karen Swallow Prior, interview with Heather Thompson Day, *Viral Jesus*, audio podcast, August 26, 2021, https://www.christianitytoday.com/ct/podcasts/viral-jesus/work-is-platform-karen-swallow-prior.html.
6. https://www.merriam-webster.com/dictionary/advocate.
7. Jentezen Franklin, *The Fasting Edge* (Lake Mary, FL: Charisma House, 201), 52.

Week Four

1. Jobes,157.
2. Debra Reid, *Esther* (Nottingham, England: InterVarsity Press Academic, 2008), 111.
3. Lynn Cowell, *Fearless Women of the Bible* (Grand Rapids, MI: Zondervan, 2022), 21.
4. https://biblehub.com/commentaries/benson/esther/5.htm.
5. https://quarterly.gospelinlife.com/justice-in-the-bible/.
6. "An American Lent; Voice of Protest and voices of Reason Reflection" by Reverend Sylvester "Tee" Turner; https://repentanceproject.org/wp-content/uploads/2020/02/AnAmericanLent.pdf.
7. https://www.history.com/topics/ancient-history/hammurabi.

8. https://quarterly.gospelinlife.com/justice-in-the-bible/.
9. Derek Kidner, *Psalms 1–72: An Introduction and Commentary* (Downer's Grove, IL: InterVarsity Press, 1973), 161.
10. https://biblehub.com/commentaries/benson/esther/5.htm.
11. Jobes, 145.
12. Jobes, 145.
13. https://biblehub.com/hebrew/5612.htm.
14. Eric Ortlund, *ESV Expository Commentary (Volume 4): Ezra–Job* (Wheaton, IL: Crossway Publishing, 2020), 272.
15. Reid, 114.
16. ESV Study Bible, 858.
17. ESV Study Bible, 2258.
18. https://today.yougov.com/opi/surveys/results#/survey/7155be60-cd19-11e6-97fe-5a944b3c4ea1/question/b5e3f1f0-cd19-11e6-97fe-5a944b3c4ea1/toplines.
19. Jobes, 152.
20. Jobes, 152–153.
21. Henri J.M. Nouwen, *The Inner Voice of Love* (New York City, NY: Random House), 32–33.
22. Jobes, 153.
23. https://www.dictionary.com/browse/whatever.
24. Jobes, 158.
25. Ortlund, 274.
26. Jobes, 161.

Week Five

1. Bill and Kristi Gualtiere, *Journey of the Soul* (Grand Rapids, MI: Baker Publishing Group, 2021), 43.
2. Michele O'Leary, Comment on, amycarroll.org, "Partnerships for Speaking Up," 3.18.21, https://amycarroll.org/partnerships-for-speaking-up/.
3. World Bank, "Poverty Overview," 10.14.2021, https://www.worldbank.org/en/topic/poverty/overview.
4. Dan Brennan, "Signs of Spiritual Abuse," Web MD, Dec. 1, 2020.
5. Emily Maust Wood "20 Influential Quotes by Dietrich Bonhoeffer," Crosswalk.com, March 4, 2021, https://www.crosswalk.com/faith/spiritual-life/inspiring-quotes/20-influential-quotes-by-dietrich-bonhoeffer.html.

6. McKinley, John, "Necessary Allies: God as Ezer, Woman as Ezer," (paper presented at the Annual Meeting of the Evangelical Theological Society, Atlanta, GA, November 17, 2015), mp3 download, 38:35, www.wordmp3.com/derails.aspx?id=20759.
7. https://www.lexico.com/en/definition/tradent.

Week Six

1. Jobes, 206.
2. https://www.ligonier.org/blog/what-providence.
3. Jobes, 195.
4. Jobes, 200.
5. Carey A. Moore, *Esther*, AB (New York: Doubleday, 1971), 88.
6. Jobes, 202.
7. Jobes, 201.
8. Jobes, 202.
9. Jobes, 202.
10. https://biblehub.com/topical/p/plunder.htm.
11. Jobes, 196.
12. Jobes, 214.
13. English Standard Version Study Bible, 856.
14. Numbers 26:55, 34:13; Joshua 7:14, 7:18; 18:6; 1 Chronicles 24:3, 24:5, 24:19.
15. https://www.biblestudytools.com/dictionary/lot/.
16. https://www.macmillandictionary.com/dictionary/british/someone-s-lot-in-life.
17. Jobes, 214.
18. https://www.chabad.org/holidays/purim/article_cdo/aid/1362/jewish/How-to-Celebrate-Purim.htm#The).
19. https://www.christianity.com/church/church-life/what-is-ash-wednesday-why-do-christians-celebrate-it.html.
20. Jobes, 221.

From the Publisher

GREAT STUDIES

ARE EVEN BETTER WHEN THEY'RE SHARED!

Help others find this study:

- Post a review at your favorite online bookseller.
- Post a picture on a social media account and share why you enjoyed it.
- Send a note to a friend who would also love it—or, better yet, go through it with them.

Thanks for helping others grow their faith!

EXODUS

Stop Walking in Circles and Reach God's Destination for Your Life

Rebecca Bender

In this study, Rebecca takes you straight into the book of Exodus where the Israelites are wandering after their own tracks immediately after escaping from bondage and oppression at the hands of Pharaoh. God is trying to get them to the land of his promise, but they, like many of us, are frustrated by doubts, fears, and self-destructive habits.

1 JOHN

Walking in the Fullness of God's Love

Wendy Blight

In this in-depth study of the book of 1 John, Wendy shares the unique insights and wisdom of the last disciple to walk with Jesus. Wendy wrote this book for every woman longing to live out God's unconditional love.

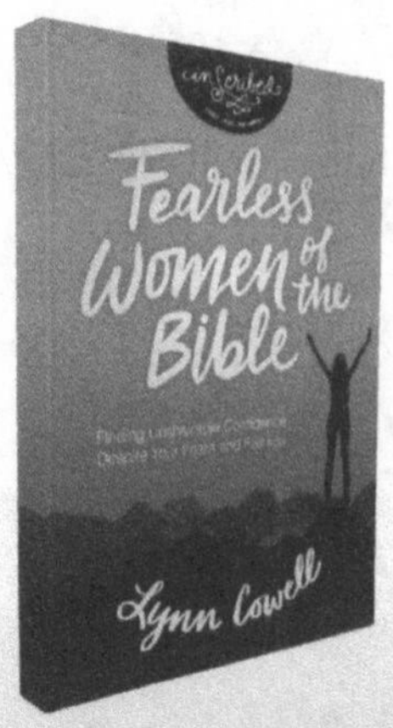

Coming Soon

ChurchSource.com/Inscribed

Know the Truth. Live the Truth. It changes everything.

If you were inspired by this study and desire to deepen your own personal relationship with Jesus Christ, Proverbs 31 Ministries has just what you are looking for.

Proverbs 31 Ministries exists to be a trusted friend who will take you by the hand and walk by your side, leading you one step closer to the heart of God through:

- Free online daily devotions
- First 5 Bible study app
- Online Bible studies
- Podcast
- COMPEL writer training
- She Speaks Conference
- Books and resources

Our desire is to help you to know the Truth and live the Truth. Because when you do, it changes everything.

For more information about Proverbs 31 Ministries, visit: www.Proverbs31.org.